Accessories
for Harley-Davidson® Motorcycles

Accessories
for Harley-Davidson® Motorcycles

Marc Cook

Design by Tom Morgan

 DAVID BULL PUBLISHING

First Printing.

Library of Congress Cataloging-in-Publication Data
    Cook, Marc.
        Accessories for Harley-Davidson motorcycles /
        Marc Cook.
            p.   cm.
        ISBN 0-9649722-7-1 (hardcover)
        1. Harley-Davidson motorcycle—Customizing. 2.
Harley-Davidson motorcycle—Equipment and supplies. I.
Title.
    TL448.H3C59 1998
    629.28'775—dc21   98-26271
                                           CIP

Book and cover design:
Tom Morgan, Blue Design, San Francisco, California.

Printed in Hong Kong.

David Bull Publishing
4250 East Camelback Road
Suite K150
Phoenix, AZ 85018
602-852-9500 / 602-852-9503 (fax)
www.bullpublishing.com

Page 2-3: At the big motorcycle shows like Daytona, you'll find a stunning variety of custom touches as well as displays from the leading vendors. These events are a great way to see your ideas in metal.

Page 4: Turn signals inset into the lower triple clamp achieve an integrated look. Most manufacturers list these items as "auxiliary" or marker lights to circumvent liability. This is Pro-One's triple-clamp set; notice also that the stanchion-tube hardware is hidden on the back side of the clamp.

Page 8: A gleaming billet instrument panel greets you. At the heart of Harley customizing is the concept that good can easily be made great and that there should be no room for boring motorcycles. Whether your addiction turns to chrome or wicked paint, chances are you can find your place with a custom Harley.

You Want Genuine Harley-Davidson Parts for Your Harley-Davidson

Acknowledgments

Harleys invoke passions, including deep devotion among those who consider the act of modifying and maintaining the bikes an art form. There are mechanics and shops for whom good enough isn't—and their dedication to doing the job right helped make them huge assets to the research for this book.

Technical Advisor Bruce Fischer is a genuine craftsman who runs a small but busy shop called Accu-True in Costa Mesa, California; Bruce is often the contrarian but his views are at least well backed in experience and a broad view of what makes a machine go fast. Other small independent shops provided similarly invaluable assistance, including South Bay Cycles in Hermosa Beach, California; HK Cycles in Livermore, California; Ron's Custom Painting in Hayward, California; Larry Hardy's Hardy Heads of Costa Mesa; and Arlen Ness Enterprises in San Leandro, California.

Among the Harley dealers who helped with the assemblage of this work are Bartels' Harley-Davidson in Marina Del Rey, California; Los Angeles Harley-Davidson in Paramount, California; Orange County Harley-Davidson in El Toro, California.

A nod of thanks to The Harley-Davidson Motor Company for opening the doors to its archives and Parts & Accessories division for an inside look at how accessories are done in house.

Finally, a heartfelt thanks to all the Harley enthusiasts who gave generously of their time and experiences so this book can be the most realistic and best photographed you'll find.

Contents

Chapter 1:

Where It All Begins

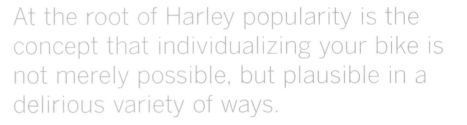

At the root of Harley popularity is the concept that individualizing your bike is not merely possible, but plausible in a delirious variety of ways.

Harley-Davidson motorcycles are like no other consumer product on Earth. No other goods have as much personality, or as devoted a following, as this brand of motorcycle. Perhaps it's because Harley has, more than any other company, been true to its own history. Compared with other vehicle manufacturers, Harley moves at a gentler pace, holding on to styling themes and mechanical pieces that the shortsighted and sup-posedly forward thinking would have discarded years back—and this is a point of pride for Harley. Adherence to its own history, to be faithful to what has made a Harley a Harley for 95 years, is dominant in the minds of stylists and engineers in Milwaukee. And it has paid off in a motorcycle line that everyone has tried to emulate but that no one can duplicate.

Harleys are about individuality, about the connection between human and machine that extends beyond the payment book and name printed on the registration card. At the root of Harley popularity is the concept that individualizing your bike is not merely possible, but plausible in a delirious variety of ways. It's not an overstatement to say that your imagination is the only limiting factor in the ways of customization.

Opposite: There's nothing like showing the world that your bike is your own. This FL-based custom sports not just wild bull horns but also a variety of cosmetic alterations and mechanical hop-ups. There would be no trouble picking this bike out of a crowded parking lot.

Above: Part of the customizing credo is to do what others say you can't, including putting a wild flame paint job on what should be a sedate touring rig. So-called baggers often are given outlandish paint and powerful engines that cast aside all pretense of being unexciting pavement pounders.

Left: A recent FLHR Road King gets a subtle brightening treatment. This set of handmade spun and chromed aluminum replaces the stock components. Also, note the chrome Allen hardware that has replaced the standard zinc-plated fasteners on the outer primary cover.

Customizing Harleys isn't *just* good fun—though it is that—but more a way of life for the devotees: By subtly—or not so subtly—changing the looks of your bike, you can make a personal statement of what's important to you, what pleases your eye most. You may choose to take your bike further back into the previous generations of Harleys, to something you, your father, or your grandfather might have ridden in bygone days. Or you could go the clean custom look, eschewing any part that doesn't make the bike look great or go down the road.

Customizing or accessorizing your Harley can be easy or hard. Given half a chance, experienced modifiers will regale you with mistakes made and tours of alteration side roads that dead-ended before they caught the highway.

Going for the complete nostalgic look, the owner of this Heritage Softail fitted it with light visors, a Panhead-style horn cover, full brake-rotor covers with chrome caliper covers, and a nifty set of fishtail muffler ends—all from Harley's Parts & Accessories division.

It's not that accessorizing your bike is difficult *per se,* but there are plenty of small ways to be led astray, and one peek at the overflowing catalog pages can be daunting, to say the least.

To assist you in making intelligent decisions in the accessorizing of your Harley, each section in this book deals with particular areas of modification.

- **Nonfunctional cosmetics.** Bolt-on items can help change the look of your bike without compromising its performance or handling, making this style of modification what the manufacturers call "parking lot mods." [see page 10]
- **Paint.** Perhaps no other single alteration will as dramatically change the look of your bike as a new paint job. We'll guide you through the process of picking the right painter and deciding on the right paint scheme.
- **Seats.** As a styling element, the seat is a surprisingly big player. Moreover, it has the potential to greatly improve the riding comfort of your bike.
- **Handlebars and foot controls.** Another link in the ergonomic chain that can give you a personalized riding position as well as distinguish your bike stylistically.
- **Engine performance upgrades.** A few well-considered changes to your Harley's powerplant can bring out a huge increase in reliable, usable power. We'll show you how to go about making the right decisions.

- **Wheels and brakes.** These are prime places to set your style and to improve the performance of your bike.
- **Suspension.** Revising or replacing your Harley's suspension will allow you to achieve a certain look, or to tailor the bike for your kind of riding and the quality of roads you travel.

A few caveats before we begin, however.

Harleys are, as Hunter Thompson might say, not like the others. While it's true that there's great overlap in models, engines, frames, and so on, there's never any hard-and-fast guarantee that every aftermarket part for a particular model will fit every *model year* bike to perfection. There are too many seemingly minor year-to-year alterations—made by Harley to improve quality or to reduce production costs—to offer any iron-clad assurance of success, so be prepared to do a little tinkering.

Be honest about your own mechanical abilities. If you've never seen the inside of an internal-combustion engine before, it's maybe not the ideal time to start by installing a new camshaft.

Watch enough of the Daytona parade and you'll soon see the popular styling trends as well as the most common bolt-on components. Don't be shy: Ask riders what they think of certain products. They're most often happy to share their opinions.

Seek expert advice. Consult with other owners, dealership personnel, and technical support people from the aftermarket itself. Avail yourself of the multiplicity of weekend rides sponsored by various Harley Owners Groups. You'll find a wealth of information and scores of rolling inspirations at just about every event. Try Daytona in the spring or Sturgis in the summer. The experience is worth the trip.

Know the Players

The Harley aftermarket is filled with suppliers large and small, including the Motor Company itself. You'll hear names like Custom Chrome, Chrome Specialties (now owned by Custom Chrome's parent company), Drag Specialties, Kury Akyn, Nempco, White Brothers, and Harley-Davidson's own Parts & Accessories division. Within the pages of these companies' catalogs you'll find dozens more independent manufacturers—for which these large houses are distributors—as well as a number of house brands that are custom manufactured for these distributors.

Harley dealers often sell a smattering of products from the aftermarket distributors and are sure to have the full H-D P&A catalog of items for sale. Smaller, independent speed shops are likely to have a main supplier—like Custom Chrome, Drag Specialties, or Nempco—but can usually get

Below: With a healthy selection of aftermarket items, this Dyna Low Rider is both faster and overall more capable than the stock version. Twin Performance Machine–built Arlen Ness calipers grip stock disks, and a Mikuni carburetor feeds the stock-displacement engine, while Drag Specialties' Python staggered duals handle the exhaust.

Above: **A Dyna Super Glide sports a good cross section of bolt-on items, including Cycle Shack staggered dual exhausts, Harley's Profile Low rear shocks, Kury Akyn footpegs, caliper inserts, and a Mikuni HRS 42 carburetor. The disk rear wheel is a standard Softail item that's been retrofitted to the Dyna.**

wares from any of the suppliers. This is an important point. If you are set on a particular product from a particular distributor, and your independent shop is hesitant to recommend the piece, find out why. It could be that they don't have as good a relationship with the vendor, or that there's some subtext. Endeavor to find out why a certain shop recommends a particular item or manufacturer.

A fully decked-out Heritage Softail. It has a raft of
Arlen Ness items, including fender rails, turn signals
in a sleek nacelle below the taillight, and a lay down
license plate holder. With an S&S carburetor and
short drag pipes, this bike is sure to make an acous-
tic impression.

"We're pretty certain that for the 1903 model, the brothers sold stick-on letters so that you could put your initials on the tank."

Vision Quest

It may sound trite, but it's true: Harley customizing starts with vision. Customizers and aftermarket producers relate a similar story time and again. New customer buys a bike and starts down the customizing path like a drunken sailor. Billet doodads here, satin finish there, a bit of chrome over there, and maybe some black powdercoat up here. The result is a new, shiny junkyard dog—a mishmash of themes and styling elements that not only fail to gel, but aggressively offend the eye.

"We've seen a lot of horror shows," one prominent customizer says. "They're never pretty and seldom cheap. Often, the best cure is to start over."

So, think long and hard about what you want the bike to be when you're at the far end of the customizing trail. An all-black Bad Boy with fat tires and a menacing look? Flames everywhere and a chopper front end? The nostalgic look and feel of a classic Electra Glide, maybe? An XR-series flat-track racer replica, perhaps? Then, snatch up the catalogs, check in with your local dealer or independent shop, take in the bike shows, and see what's happening.

Through all this, the emphasis should be on making a personal statement without hobbling your motorcycle as a piece of transportation. Thanks to Harley's fantastic resurgence and newfound corpo-

Opposite: Harley has been making accessories for its own motorcycles almost since the beginning. By the 1940s, its captive aftermarket division was booming; it continues unprecedented growth today.

rate vigor, the bikes themselves need make few apologies in terms of function. Our goal is to retain all that's good in a Harley—an iconoclastic yet instantly identifiable American look and that elusive quality known as "character"—but give you the tools to make intelligent modification decisions you'll still be happy with into the next millennium.

Let's Get Started: Bolt-on Bliss

Talk to enough customizers, and you'll think that reworking the looks of a Harley is a relatively recent phenomenon. Not true. According to Martin Jack Rosenblum, Harley-Davidson's official historian, customizing touches have been around as long as Harleys themselves. "We're pretty certain that for the 1903 model, the brothers sold stick-on letters so that you could put your initials on the tank," says Rosenblum. Beyond that simplistic bit of customizing, you could argue that even the first Harley-Davidsons could be factory customized. "The first few model years of bikes didn't come with fenders, so the company sold them as options," says Rosenblum.

As the bikes progressed in size and capability, so did the accessories available for them. At first, the items were primarily aimed at improving performance or extending utility—things like luggage racks, rearview mirrors, additional lighting. "But the parts also had an element of visual embellishment," says Rosenblum. "They weren't just for go, nor were they just for show."

Above: **Sometimes you just need a place for keys or a pack of gum. This Harley P&A tank pouch for the Bad Boy Softail provides a visual link between the speedometer and forward edge of the seat.**

Storz Performance produces a fiberglass body kit for Softails that replaces the stock seat and rear fender. Except for the need to paint it, it is basically a bolt-on kit.

Now It's Your Turn

Before embarking on this customizing excursion, you should form some idea of how far you want to go. Is your goal to make light modifications that will only reveal themselves to the dyed-in-the-wool Harley buff? Or do you want the modifications to have a thorough, can't-miss-it, in-your-face effect on passersby? Are you a fanatic for flames, or maybe more interested in the scalloped billet pieces? Take your time and look over the accessorized bikes you'll find at shows, in the parking lot, and at the local weekend ride.

Recognize, too, that among all the bikes modified—and, yes, there are still a few stock Harleys running around out there—by far the vast majority are mild custom cases. Works of art from the prolific and highly visible customizers represent just a small percentage of all the bikes on the road. Don't think that you have to tread in their esteemed steps lest you get ostracized from your local Harley hangout on the weekend. Instead, the aim here ought to be to create a distinctive bike, one that mirrors your taste and sense of style.

Occasionally the top-line customizers make a big deal about never "copying another guy's design."

Left: **Another Storz kit turns an ordinary XL into a mix between a dirt-track refugee and a British sportbike. The hand-formed fuel tank mates with a new fiberglass tail section and seat support. Because of the need to prep and paint both an aluminum tank and composite tailsection, this kit requires the services of experienced hands.**

Below: Reworking the lighting is straightforward. Here, colored inserts give the classic spotlights on this customized FL a high-tech look. The tri-bar headlight and billet running lights are from Weekend Concepts.

Right: This Softail's eye-catching appearance is largely the result of bolt-on components, including replacement fender rails and a running-light insert from Harley P&A, a Kury Akyn mask (which also has famous blue-dot inserts) for the stock taillight, Arlen Ness's chrome radius license plate frame, and chassis dress-up items like Harley's axle-adjuster covers.

And while it's admirable that these big guns profess to follow only their own visions, there's no reason you can't pick and choose from what other riders have done. Remember, this is *your* bike, and you can do anything to it that you please. Don't be bullied.

Honing the Visuals

Reflecting the company's down-to-earth Midwestern roots, much of what you see on a current bike, hardware-wise, is intended to do the job without much embellishment. And unlike many other brands of bikes, Harleys have minimal bodywork.

This presents a problem of sorts for a manufacturer. Sure, you want every part of the motorcycle to be artwork—fasteners and clamps that are so beautiful and stunningly rendered that you'd worry about throwing a wrench over them. But the production realities are quite different, as are concerns for durability. That's why much of what you'll see

1. Smaller turn signals contrasted with the large stock Harley items help clean up the rear of the bike.

2. Another way to alter the bike's frontal area is to use small turn signals that bolt to the fork stanchions. Be forewarned that these small lights do not meet the highway standards of the stock items for light-to-light width or output. It's extremely uncommon to be cited for such a change, however. You may also need a load equalizer to keep the standard turn signal canceler working properly.

3. Harley P&A visors adorn the headlight and turn signal lenses; the directionals have been relocated to the fork stanchions with a Drag Specialties kit. They normally live on the lever perches.

This Softail uses a combination of chromed and ball-milled (a style of making indents in billet material) derby cover and inspection plate from Custom Chrome mated with chromed frame side rails to dramatically brighten an otherwise dark motorcycle.

Chrome Exchange:
Should You or Shouldn't You?

It's become popular for Harley-Davidson dealers and independent shops to build inventory in common parts, have them chromed, and offer them on an exchange basis for the stock polished items. Is this a good idea?

The answer is a conclusive *it depends*. First, you have to know what you're looking at. If, for example, you can positively identify an abused or out-of-date part, and can quickly determine the quality of the chrome job, then the exchange setup can offer a quick and relatively painless turnaround.

If you can't tell one part from the next by sight, or you are concerned about trading in a new part for one with an unknown pedigree, then you are best off having your own components sent to the polisher or chromer. It may take a bit longer—you may have to miss a weekend's ride—but for most shadetree customizers, it's the safest bet.

on a Harley is built for ease of construction and long-term life—items like zinc-plated fasteners, die-cast steel covers instead of brightly chromed billet pieces, simple stampings in places like the belt-tensioner end plates. Those ultracustom bits of decoration you'll find on show-winning bikes are seldom—though not necessarily never—found on the out-of-the-crate machines.

This kind of mechanical simplicity has opened the door for the aftermarket and adorned its welcome mat with gold. Where the big custom-part distributors and manufacturers once specialized in basic replacement items and go-fast parts, the majority these days concentrate on cosmetic alterations—they spend much more time defining upcoming trends and working CNC machines day and night on derby covers and fork crowns.

Common Lines

Something else has helped set off the great aftermarket explosion—Harley's tremendous parts commonality. For example, a major accessory like a primary cover will, with some modifications, fit just about every Big Twin produced in the past decade. Likewise, Harley has used the same basic frame designs for a very long time—the newest, the Dyna Glide, which replaced the venerable FXR series, debuted in 1991. So it's possible for small manufacturers to tool up for accessories and know they have a large market. They also know that it's unlikely that Harley will shift courses overnight.

It's also worth noting that the custom-bike artisans really don't intend their offspring to be daily riders—despite oft-heard protestations to the contrary. Find a guy with a big-bucks custom and you'll probably also espy a less-extravagant Harley in his garage that is his routine mount. Save the heavy chrome and four-digit paint job for Saturday morning, or so goes the theory.

1. **Harley classifies its finishes by grade. A stock Dyna Wide Glide's lower triple clamp actually has two classes of finish. The upper section that is easily seen is polished and partly covered with a chromed-steel plate. The lower portion, which you would not normally see, is left in the as-cast condition.**

2. **All Evolution Big Twin and Sportster models use three-tier rocker boxes; this gives the aftermarket plenty of opportunities to make distinctive replacements with either one part of the sandwich or all three. Always use new gaskets when opening or replacing the rocker boxes. They're cheap, and fixing an oozing cover can be a real pain.**

3. **Standard Harley head bolts aren't exactly sublime. Joker Machine makes a billet cover that slips over the stock item.**

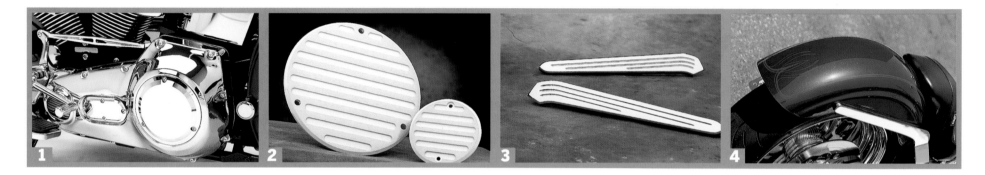

1. **Joker Machine makes a wide line of billet accessories, including this set, which features a smooth derby cover and inspection panel. These are strictly bolt-on items and take the place of the stock components without the need to modify the bike.**

2. **Shown here in white, Harley Parts & Accessories division's own derby and timing-cover kits are matched components that can be ordered with one of several trim paint choices for both Big Twins and Sportsters.**

3. **Arlen Ness's chrome billet side rails use hidden fasteners for the cleanest possible look. Be cautious installing this style of fender rail—regardless of manufacturer—when also using a wider-than-stock rear tire.**

4. **Sleek side rails really help create a smooth, seamless rear view. A reverse of the standard Harley arrangement, this setup uses hardware inserted from the tire side of the fender. As a result, it's important to be careful when fitting a larger rear tire because this hardware inevitably protrudes. It also makes getting a tool onto the fastener more difficult.**

So the great masses of Harleys in this world receive far less customizing than do the ultra customs. It is also within this arena—in the so-called bolt-on customizing—that most riders begin their modification journey. It makes sense. Virtually all of the bolt-on custom touches can be installed with little effort and only a modicum of mechanical ability. You don't need to know how to paint or weld to personalize your bike. Moreover, the bolt-on segment of the aftermarket has the most players and the greatest variety of parts.

There are some other good reasons for starting with bolt-on accessories. For one, they are very often reversible. Should you change your mind about, say, flamed custom bits, you can always go back to stock or set out on another stylistic theme.

Motor, As in Motorcycle

Naturally, the Harley-Davidson engine—whether 883cc, 1200cc, or 1340cc—is unlike any other. With an included angle of 45 degrees and inline cylinder bores—not offset side-to-side as with the other V-twins on the market—the Harley powerplant is instantly recognizable to even a

Left: A standard Road King chrome headlight nacelle is dressed up with a 50's Boy billet light ring.

Below: Arlen Ness's signature derby cover is a work of CNC-machined art. Cut-from-billet construction means the Ness piece is probably stronger (and heavier) than the original component. It fits most Big Twin models.

Bottom: Arlen Ness's billet oil-filter cover slips over standard and aftermarket spin-on filter elements. Small set screws keep the cover in place. Given that the oil filter is prominently located on both the Big Twin and Sportster models, this add-on is an effective way to provide an extra bit of glamour to your bike.

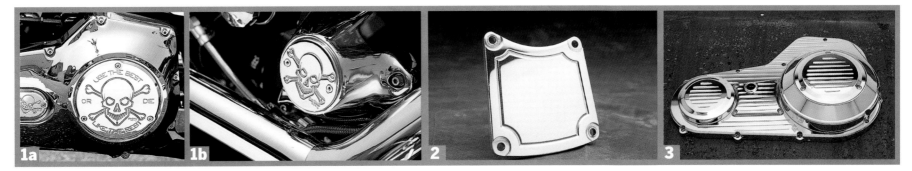

1a. **Skull-and-crossbones themes remain popular in Harleydom. Here, Bad Bones's "buy the best" billet cover set has been added to a Softail.** 1b. **Bad Bones's matching skull-and-crossbones billet timing cover plate completes the ensemble. Notice that this cover mounts with a set of small Allen-head screws instead of the standard Harley aluminum rivets. This greatly improves access to the ignition sender.**

2. **Performance Machine builds a billet inspection plate. The groove cut into the outer edge is to set this piece apart from the simple stock item.**

3. **If replacing the primary driver covers isn't enough for you, you might want to use a whole new outer primary cover. This Joker Machine piece fits FXR models with midmount foot controls**

Opposite: **Harley's Aluminator line includes engine dress-up items like this transmission end cover and oil dipstick. This is Harley's foray into machined-from-billet componentry. The company says that it will expand the line as the market demands but feels that its traditional die-cast and stamped bolt-ons are better suited to long-term use.**

neophyte. And because the basic Big Twin Evolution engine—stock size of 1340cc, or 80 cubic inches—has been the mainstay of the firm's lineup for more than a decade, there are pieces aplenty for it. The Big Twin's smaller brother, the Evolution Sportster engine, has been around nearly as long and possesses almost as great a variety of parts.

When most owners start the customizing tour, they begin by dressing up the engine. Probably the single most popular part is called the derby cover. This is simply a disk-shaped inspection cover on the gearbox end of the primary drive. Three bolts hold this cover in place, so popping off the stocker and replacing it with a custom billet or stamped steel piece is a true five-minute cinch. (We'll talk about specifics for installation later.)

Many manufacturers of custom parts provide a line of goods with matching styling themes that fit a variety of the engine parts—rocker-box covers, inspection panels, air-cleaner covers, points covers (the small plate at the crankshaft line on the right side of the Evolution Big Twin), transmission covers, and so on. Why change? For the most part, the stock Harley parts here are simply polished aluminum

1. Custom Chrome sells this oil-filter boss cover. Normally, you'd see a pair of oil lines against the wrinkle-black or unpainted, as-cast finish (depending on how your bike came from the factory) engine cases. Covers have become increasingly popular because the underlying system remains untouched and the look can be changed at will.

2. Harley P&A's V-wing derby cover is made in the same die-cast aluminum as the original cover, and fits late-model Big Twins. Similarly styled covers are also available for Evolution Sportsters.

3. Old Harley-style taillight and downsized turn signals from Drag Specialties help clean up the rear fender and give the bike a set-apart style. This 1960s- and 1970s-era Harley part is an appealing alternative to the all-plastic taillight used on all but three Harley models.

pieces—nothing dowdy, but hardly pulse-quickening either. Besides, the presence of the engine in a Harley is large, so modification dollars spent here reap big rewards.

Custom Chrome, for example, has developed a line of add-on bits called the Inferno line. Naturally, if you like flames, you'll love this stuff. Purely cosmetic additions dot this lineup like a teenager's face after a chocolate binge—you've got airbox covers, bolt-on dress-ups for all of the major engine covers, nut and bolt covers, axle adornments, and other chassis items like mirrors and fuel caps.

Quality Check

Because most of these bolt-on parts are purely cosmetic, your demands on their quality can be somewhat more lax than for the mechanically important stuff. Within this group of bolt-on parts, there are two distinct types: the parts that cover or replace some noncritical part, and those that replace panels or outer cases that could leak or create other kinds of mechanical mayhem. You need to pay much closer attention to the quality of parts in the second category than in the first.

That does not mean, however, that just any cheap part will do, even for the noncritical items. As with anything you want to put on your bike, you should consider buying from the established makers first—many of these companies or distributors have reputations to nurture and the economic wherewithal to back up warranty claims with more than a grunt and a "get outta here." Also, ask at your local dealership or speed shop what they've had the best luck with. According to Steve Constantine, owner of South Bay Cycles in Hermosa Beach, California, "There is a lot of junk out there. We could sell it, but eventually the poor-quality parts come back to us and we have to make the situation right. Buy the good stuff the first time out."

How Does It Look?

Always start with appearances. Take the part you're considering out to your bike and see how the chrome matches the other chrome on the bike. There are two main types of chrome finishes, one bluish and the other somewhat yellowish. You often can't tell which is which without comparing your new part to the chrome already on your bike.

(Harley chrome, for reference, is most often the better-quality bluish type and is by all accounts exceptionally well applied given the number of parts the company turns out.)

When examining replacement inspection covers and purely cosmetic panels, make sure the dimensions are correct. If possible, take the new part out of the packaging and place it side-by-side with your factory part. Are the bolts in the same place, and are there the same number of them? Do the corners and rounded edges match the openings in your cases properly? Are the back sides of cast and thin-metal items ribbed or otherwise supported? If you're buying a billet-aluminum replacement for a factory die-cast part—which tends to be thicker and heavier—will your stock hardware work? Does this kit include new bolts if the stockers won't work? In many cases, the difference between a $20 part and a $45 part is that extra casting or machining process that adds durability.

Other engine dress-up items include airbox covers—just make sure you have the right part for your model-year bike—as well as coil and horn covers. The general rule here is that the new part should as closely as possible mimic the shape and heft of the old. Don't be surprised if a part marked, for instance, to fit a 1987 to 1994 FXR doesn't mesh seamlessly on your 1991 FXR—Harley did and does make year-to-year changes that many of the aftermarket companies either can't or won't follow.

Top left: This bolt-on turn signal set from Drag Specialties employs a 90-degree adapter that allows them to be placed horizontally. Replacement lenses can be purchased in red or amber.

Middle left: Small-lens turn signals are available from Harley. They use smaller, shallower bulbs to allow the lens to fit snugly against the stock backing bucket.

Bottom left: A chrome headlight nacelle is sufficiently sleek, but these small marker lights (by Drag Specialties) help keep the front end uncluttered.

Chrome and Polish:
Inside the Glamour Tweaks

Two of the most popular methods of dressing up motorcycle parts—by chroming or polishing—in fact have their roots in preservation. Bare aluminum surfaces—of which most of your Harley is constructed, the "Milwaukee Iron" nickname notwithstanding—will by themselves suffer surface oxidation when exposed to the atmosphere. Which is to say, pretty much at any time.

Polishing is the act of smoothing the surface of the metal with an abrasive. By dramatically reducing the surface roughness, the part will be far more reflective. Most of Harley's original outer cases are polished to a medium luster and then coated to prevent surface corrosion. Eventually, though, this layer will deteriorate and the surface will become dull. In fact, this means that the

aluminum has formed its own protective layer of corrosion, so further degradation will not occur and the part's integrity will not be compromised. Sure looks crummy, though.

Many companies will, for a fee, further polish various parts of your bike to a much higher state of shine. This approach is used often by veteran customizers, so the outcome is well known. Indeed, there's little danger in having the cosmetic parts of your bike polished by an experienced shop. (Make certain the shop understands that it should never polish any surface that mates to another, like the flange of the primary case. The gasket used between

these surfaces depends on a certain degree of roughness to provide a good seal.) Always opt for a high-quality clearcoat after the polishing, unless you really enjoy spending an hour polishing for every hour you intend to ride.

Chroming is another method of cranking up the surface brightness, but it's a totally different process. It is more correctly called a plating process. It's a

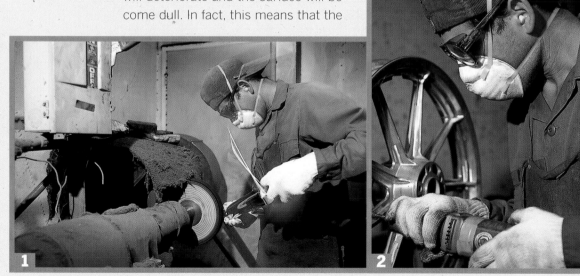

1. **Every chrome job begins with polishing the part to a fine luster. This helps seal in impurities in castings and prevents the subsequent platings from "dropping into" minute surface imperfections in the material.**
2. **Cast wheels particularly must be carefully polished to seal the surface and provide a smooth face for the nickel and chrome plates.**
3. **Chroming hardware requires careful preparation as well, especially to keep from losing anything.**

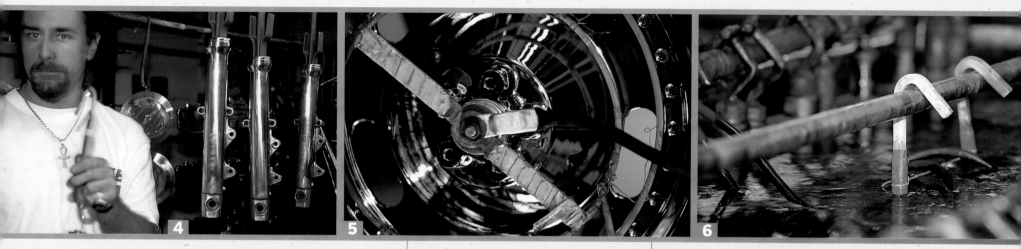

tricky, difficult method of plating that takes skilled workers to do well. Moreover, there are myriad tricks employed by the high-end chrome shops to make sure the coverage of the chrome on any part is as uniform as possible.

Chris Hill, general manager for the motorcycle division of South Bay Chrome in Costa Mesa, California, says there are three main questions you should ask of any chrome shop. "First, how long has the shop been in business? A guy who's just starting has a lot of learning to do. Second, what kind of guarantee does the work include? We offer a year; some shops only guarantee the surface for three or six months. We also chrome bumpers and offer a lifetime guarantee to the original purchaser. You have to have confidence in your work to do that. Third, find out how the chromer tracks the parts. You don't want to get someone else's switch housings because you don't

know if they've been abused or how old they are. We photograph every part that comes in for identification and keep the work order separate throughout the chroming process."

Proper chroming is indeed a process. It starts with a thorough cleaning of the parts. Chromed parts will require one kind of stripper, while painted steel and aluminum need another. Once the part is down to bare metal, it goes to the polishing department. This is where the final quality of the chrome is determined. As with paint, the majority of the magic in chroming is in the preparation.

Next comes a plating of copper. This soft metal helps seal in the pores of the metal and provides a smoother surface for the following material to adhere to. If you've seen bad chrome jobs that are full of pits, you can bet that either the polishing or copper-plating job was done hurriedly.

4. Chris Hill of South Bay Chrome shows the proper way to wrap fastener threads for chroming.

5. Special anodes—which resemble pencil-thick wires and are intended to provide a positive charge near the to-be-plated surface—fit into wheels and other parts to help evenly distribute the electroplating materials.

6. When placed in the chemical bath, the item to be chromed is subjected to high-voltage, low-current electricity to promote deposition of the plating material from sacrificial anode to the item, which is the cathode.

Chrome and Polish continued . . .

Following the copper plating—which is all of .002 to .008 of an inch thick—the part returns to the polisher for additional buffing. After that, the part gets a layer of nickel plate. The type of nickel and its thickness, for the most part, determine the color of the final chrome you see.

Immediately after the nickel-plating process, the part goes into the chromic acid bath. As with the copper- and nickel-plating processes, the chrome is "thrown" onto the part through electrolysis. That is, the part being plated is wired as the cathode, or negatively

charged part, and a sacrificial anode of the plating material is wired as the anode, or positively charged component. With the application of electricity and the presence of a liquid electrolyte, the transfer of the plating material may take place.

After the chrome plating is finished, the part will be sent to the inspection table, where it will be checked for good chrome coverage and any chipping or cracking. It will then be given a protective polish or wax and be prepared for shipping back to you.

7. After being immersed in the vat for a carefully controlled amount of time, the wheel comes out with a protective nickel plating.
8. When the wheel emerges from the final chrome-deposition step, it appears almost golden in color.
9. A simple water rinse reveals the desired bluish-tint chrome.

Inside Harley-Davidson's
Parts and Accessories Division

Whatever the company line from the other aftermarketers, the fact is that Harley plays in the accessories game by a different set of rules—it has to as the original-equipment manufacturer (OEM). Harley's P&A arm is obliged to spend more time engineering and developing accessories, and it is more concerned that the parts fit properly across a wide range of model years. More importantly, the company strives to ensure that the accessories are compatible among themselves—that is, a windshield for, say, a Fat Boy must coexist with a passing-lamp kit and lower wind deflectors. This isn't as easy a task as it sounds, because to adhere to the multifit concept calls for clever mounting schemes and extensive cross-testing. "We're pretty certain that no one else in the aftermarket does as much testing as we do," says Tom Parsons, director of category management, motorcycle accessories. (That's a long title that essentially means he's the main checks and balances for new accessories.)

Another reason Harley shies away from fast-track accessory development involves product-durability testing. A good example is the firm's Detachables, a series of accessories that can turn a bike from a bare-bones street-trawler to a road-ready tourer (or nearly so) in minutes. At the heart of the Detachables is a mounting system that allows for removal of racks, windshields, backrests, and passenger seats without the use of tools. Because the mounting scheme employs pins and cams that could as easily come off on the road unintentionally as in your garage on purpose, Harley has to test each component for suitability and durability. This means, in turn, loading the racks to well above their intended weight handling capacities, and, well, going for a long ride.

1. Springer forks use a simple chrome link between the trailing suspension arm and the axle. Harley's P&A division created this chrome cover specifically for the Heritage Softail Springer based on a late 1940s design. It will fit any Heritage Springer fork.

2. Racks can make a trip across town with a load far simpler. Harley makes a special line of easily removable racks and accessories called the Detachables. Here is a rack for current XLs that slides into special carriers screwed into the stock fender rails. The rack comes off in a second or two, leaving no unsightly hardware.

3. Dyna Wide Glides have a standard short sissy bar, and this rack for the FXDWG works with all the original pieces in place.

In fact, Harley has a dedicated test facility that includes both smooth and relentlessly rough roads it can use to test accessories. Alternatively, Harley can employ a testing fixture at its headquarters R&D facility that reproduces the shakes and rattles of the road. This device can give the engineers a preview of whether or not a new accessory will shed its hardware under demanding conditions.

"By the time we've released a product for manufacturing, we're exceptionally sure that it will work and that it will hold up for the long run," says Bob Farchione, chief engineer for Harley's P&A division.

Because Harley acts like the large manufacturing concern that it is, the P&A department's production philosophies are much different from the norm. While most small manufacturers make use of computer numerically controlled (CNC) machines to crank out machined-from-stock, billet-aluminum parts, Harley does most of its work from metal castings or stampings. Tooling up for a casting or stamping is much more involved and requires considerably more lead time than for CNC-produced parts. (A hungry CNC programmer/machinist can have a part prototyped in the morning, check-fit it by lunchtime, and have a new part in production by the end of the day.) Harley says that its production methods produce better parts, at lower cost, and with greater consistency and repeatability.

Because Harley's tooling investment is so great, you will no doubt notice

that the company is quite particular about the kinds of products released through P&A. Many of the dress-up kits in the catalog are in fact production items from select models. For example, the chrome primary-chain cover sold for mainline Sportsters are the same parts put on the Sportster Custom on the regular assembly line.

Such a product tactic, obviously, has benefits and weaknesses. First, the parts are likely to be quite conservative in nature, with little of the flash and trend-setting style that is a big selling point of the more flexible accessory manufacturers. On the other hand, you have greater assurance that the parts will fit; after all, they are basically cosmetically altered versions of the same part that's already on the bike. Ask the owner of any small (non–Harley dealership) shop, and he'll probably tell you that the Harley-Davidson P&A pieces almost always fit without complications.

Among the prime mix-and-match components Harley sells through its ac-

4. In celebration of its 95th birthday in 1998, Harley produced commemorative bolt-on pieces. This 95th air-cleaner insert and timing cover adorn an otherwise stock bike.

5. Harley's tombstone taillight has been an enduring classic. Harley's version is almost identical to the 1940s part from which it's derived.

cessories catalog are engine dress-up kits. These are usually chromed components that may be simply polished aluminum on your model—rocker-boxes, primary covers, camshaft covers, derby covers, primary-chain inspection covers, and transmission top and end covers. Again, these parts are standard, production-line items, chromed instead of polished. You can also get chromed control levers, handlebar switch assemblies, and foot controls.

It is worthwhile to note that Harley does indeed provide these components for out-of-production models, and having the engineering data in the same building gives the P&A engineers a huge leg up on the competition. For example, Harley routinely makes subtle modifications to the running gear—sometimes these changes affect things like the fit of the primary cover, and sometimes they don't. Still, many an aftermarket producer of these parts finds out the hard way that the company has changed the location of some critical component, thereby rendering a "fits all Big Twins" part to one that only works on certain model years.

Harley has tremendous incentive to make sure the parts fit and that the applications chart is up-to-date. That's because it's very likely that a Harley

dealer will be installing the more complicated parts sold through P&A. If there are problems installing the components, the Milwaukee office will hear about it in a heartbeat.

One of the ways in which Harley is attempting to catch up with the rapidly changing customizing scene is by forming alliances with noted aftermarket manufacturers. A good example is its affiliation with Fox Racing, builders of shock absorbers for a wide range of street and dirt bikes. Harley wanted a strong partner, and got it in Fox. P&A's Profile Low Rear Suspension—available for Dyna Glide, FXR, and Sportster models —is the result of this collaboration. According to Harley, these shocks are tailored specifically for each model, more so than the original shocks.

Yet another advantage of Harley P&A's approach is that parts remain in the catalog longer than just about anyone else's line. While this may sound like scant advantage, consider what would happen if you dropped your bike and broke some critical (and aftermarket-sourced) part.

Harley is poised to take on even more of the aftermarket, according to P&A marketing man Jeff Merten. "You can expect to see a lot more new product from us," he says, "and we're work-

6. Harley's Detachables line—including this sissy bar—uses cam-style locking plates to secure the device to the bike. Harley punished these pieces in testing to ensure that they'll work for a long time. Security, however, is a concern for some riders because the Detachables can be easily removed without having to unlock anything.

7. Harley's eagle motif appears on a wide variety of bolt-on products, including the company's sissy bar insert.

8. The full-on 95th Fat Boy collection includes a Lexan windshield, special paint scheme and colors, 95th badging, and a modicum of collectability.

ing to reduce our lead times so that we'll have more new items in each future catalog." It is Harley's stated aim to have the best-produced parts in the aftermarket, and to take even greater advantage of the P&A division's proximity to the mainline engineering groups. That should send a message to the other aftermarket companies that Harley is ready and able to play in the accessorizing game. The heightened competition from such a commitment will no doubt benefit consumers.

Above: **Many of Harley's current models leave the battery exposed. A chrome cover—standard on some of the company's high-end models—helps turn an element that any other manufacturer would try to hide into a element of the bike's styling.**

Filling in the Gaps

While many of the custom pieces are designed to replace existing bits on your bike, still more are intended to be added without removing anything else. A good example of this type of accessory is the Rick Doss battery box extension for the Dyna Glide; normally, the area behind the exposed battery and in front of the fender leaves an unsightly frame member exposed. Doss's chromed steel plate simply clips onto the battery box and fills in this area.

There are several permutations of this kind of cover. Others include cover-up plates for the back of the oil-filter boss, for the oil filter itself.

Nut Covers

The name sounds like some kind of squirrel-food protection device, but nut covers are actually decorative pieces intended to hide the function-over-form nuts and bolts on your bike. For the most part, nut covers slip entirely over the fasteners—or the heads of bolts—to hide the real part. There are also inserts that fill the hexed portion of the Allen bolts used so liberally on modern Harleys; they provide a much cleaner look on exposed items like the primary cover and cam case. (Beware, those of you in wet climates. The inserts can hold water in the hex cavity and promote corrosion.)

Right: **Rick Doss's simple steel cover closes in the area between the frame and the battery box on all Dyna Glides; it's sold by Custom Chrome.**

Pulley replacement isn't necessary if you use a pulley cover, like this Harley P&A model for Softails. Note also the axle cover kit and chromed upper and lower belt guards, both from Harley.

1. Arlen Ness is known for creating artwork. This CNC-machined and chromed pulley cover replaces the mundane lower guard on Big Twins.

2. Harley P&A's chrome belt guard for Big Twins uses factory engineering to provide new-bike fit and finish.

3. Combine a chrome pulley with chrome upper and lower belt guards—these are from Harley's P&A catalog—and you will have replaced otherwise plain-finish or black-painted components. For the investment, it's hard to beat this tactic for brightening up the bike.

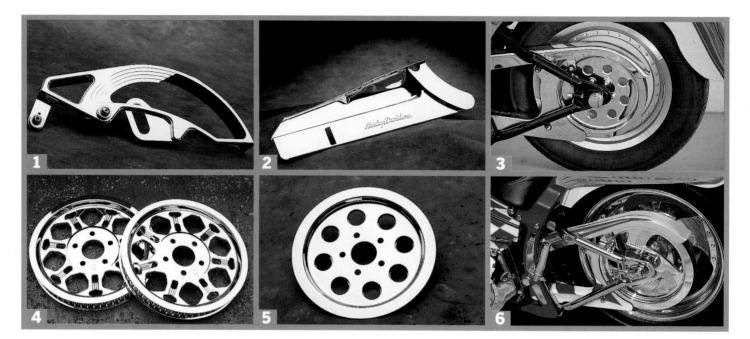

Another alternative to the hardware covers is to replace the hardware itself with chromed or otherwise customized replacements. Arlen Ness, Regency, and many others sell custom fastener kits that can really make the engine look smoother and sleeker. Such a tactic will cause no harm in non-critical areas, but you don't want to replace important bits like brake-caliper hardware, axles, or major engine bolts without knowing absolutely that the alternatives are as strong as stock.

Driveline Dress-Up

Beyond the basic engine cosmetics, you'll find replacement pieces for every part of the bike, including the transmission and final drive. Chromed or polished belt guards are very popular. You can find belt guards—both the top and lower panels—in chromed steel or billet aluminum. Most companies take pains to make the replacements fit the standard mounting holes and to clear the belt and pulleys properly. But before you ride off, make a second check to be sure that nothing gets in the way of the belt. A guard pulled into the belt will make big, expensive noises and could lock the rear wheel tight. Not the kind of payback you want in rush-hour traffic.

4. Billet rear pulleys for belt-drive models offer the opportunity to customize the entire wheel assembly. Joker Machine, among others, produces a line of wheels with styling to match these pulleys.

5. An alternative to replacing the rear pulley is to use a pulley cover, like this chrome, stamped-steel example from Harley P&A. The sole disadvantage of using a cover is that in dirty or muddy conditions grunge can get trapped between the cover and the pulley proper.

6. A Performance Machine billet pulley anchors a variety of custom touches on this Softail. A chromed swingarm is mated to chromed axle hardware. The upper and lower belt guards carry through the overall paint scheme.

Left: Performance Machine's CNC-machined billet replacement pulley is a lead-pipe cinch to dress up the rear wheel of the bike. Be certain to buy the replacement pulley with the correct number of teeth for your bike, or the gearing will be altered. You can add or subtract up to three teeth without buying a new belt.

Following that theme of belt beautifiers, you will also find a number of dress-up items for the rear pulley itself. Harley and several of the aftermarket firms sell chrome inserts that simply sit over the stock pulley. And while you will have to remove the rear wheel for installation, the alteration is not as involved as swapping out the whole pulley. If you do decide to replace the pulley whole, make sure you're getting one with the correct number of teeth. Softails have taller gearing than do the rubber-mount Dynas, FXRs, and FLTs. Similarly, a Sportster pulley is different from a Big Twin's.

Odds and Ends

As you will probably discover in perusing the catalogs, there are endless doodads and add-ons that aim to dress up the bike—things like replacement license plate brackets and billet license plate frames. Billet covers for the master cylinder reservoir are quite popular—just be sure to keep the brake fluid off the paint and make certain the inside sealing surface of the new part will accommodate the old gasket without wrinkling.

Many riders opt for replacement fuel caps in the same styling vein as the engine covers. Perhaps one of the most clever and useful of these fuel tank dress-ups are Carlini's tank savers. These chrome inserts screw into the standard tank opening and provide a protective surface around the filler neck; normally, this is just a plain painted-steel surface that is prone to nicks and scratches from gas nozzles.

Save for the touring models, Harleys don't come with a toolkit nor any convenient way to carry one. This is a clever solution: a tubular billet tool carrier from Pro-One bolted to the frame's forward downtubes.

Arlen Ness builds this hot-for-flames fuel cap. It's literally a screw-on installation.

A popular modification because it's so useful is Carlini's Paintsaver. A chrome ring fits between the filler opening and gas cap to protect the paint from scratches caused by fuel nozzles. A matching ring is available for the faux left-side gas cap on many FXR and Dyna Glide models.

1. Billet speedometer housings have become a mark of high-end customizers. This Ness piece bolts in place of the stock casting, providing quite a bit of brightwork and billet class.

2. Harley's Diamondback series of bolt-on items includes this tank-to-seat panel; it matches another panel designed to trail behind the Diamondback solo seat.

3. Harley makes this chromed instrument binnacle for certain Dyna and FXR models to replace the standard painted item. It, too, is an easy bolt-on piece.

4. Another method of visually joining the instrument binnacle and the seat is a leather insert. Many stock Harley models have such a cosmetic touch, but it can easily be added to those models that do not. The insert is held down by the instrument panel and located by the forward seat tang.

Left: Another way of carrying tools on a Harley is this teardrop-shaped kit designed for Softails and made by Harley. Based on a historic design, the box can be fitted to either side of the bike.

Opposite: A side-mount taillight pays homage to the bad-boy choppers of old. Combining the taillight and license plate frame frees the rear fender from such duties and creates a now-common custom look.

Above: **Instrument customizing is common, in part because it's so easy to do. This one-off speedo face has been removed and painted to the owner's fancy. With the help of the service manual, disassembling the speedo and doing the modification yourself is about an hour's work. You can buy off-the-shelf replacement faces from many aftermarket sources.**

Harley has introduced a series of styling elements called the Diamond Back collection. With matching seats and instrument-panel bibs, the Diamond Backs also include triangular vinyl-and-metal plates that extend over the rear fender behind a solo saddle. The tailsections both tie together the visual aspects of the bike but also hide the inevitable scratches on the rear fender if you sometimes run a dual saddle.

Ultimately, the number of purely cosmetic alterations you can perform to your bike may be limited more by imagination and time than anything else. As you'll soon discover on the winding road of Harley accessorizing, you can do just about anything you want.

Which is, after all, part and parcel of the Harley heritage.

1. **A Road King owner has spruced up the standard instrument panel with a leather inlay from Harley P&A that features black center studs. This theme is repeated on the seat valance to good effect.**

2. **Custom Chrome's turn signal relocation kit moves the stock items from their normal location under the hand-control perches to either the upper or lower triple clamp. You will have to use a special, shortened Allen wrench to tighten the upper triple clamp bolts.**

3. **By moving the turn signals from their normal, under-perch mounts, it's possible to change handlebar bends and positions without having the backs of the bullet-shaped signals touch the tank at maximum steering lock.**

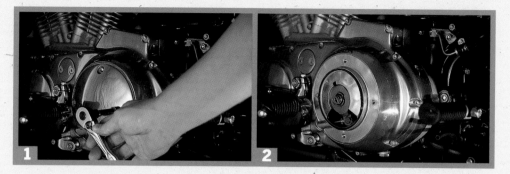

Inspection Covers Installation

Installing replacement inspection covers on the Harley engine is fairly straightforward. Just be sure to take your time, buy new gaskets (even if your bike is just a few hundred miles old), have the correct tools at hand, and, above all else, make sure the service manual is at the ready. The following describes the removal of stock derby and primary-chain inspection covers. Other covers are dealt with similarly.

1. Level the motorcycle. You can either invest in a center stand (they run about $150 to $200 for the simpler ones) or shim the sidestand so that the bike is nearly vertical. If you chose the latter option, make sure the bike is over far enough to the left so that it won't topple easily.

2. Position a drip pan under the derby cover. There will be enough fluid in the primary chain case that you might spill some; how much depends on how successful you were in leveling the bike.

3. Use your #27 Torx wrench to loosen the three button-head screws. (Some models may have 5/32-inch Allen-head bolts instead.) Note that

the washers have small rubber grommets on the inner diameter; do not substitute hardware-store washers during reassembly.

4. Remove the derby cover by gently prying at the gap around the outer circumference; be careful not to dent anything or chip the chrome.

5. Take note of the condition of the sealing O-ring that should stay in the groove in the primary cover. If it looks ragged or if there are any signs of leakage, replace it. You may not need to replace the O-ring now, but if you catch it with the screwdriver removing the cover, you'll be happy you have a spare.

6. While you're in there, take a look at the clutch basket and diaphragm spring. There should be no signs of breakage or debris floating in the primary-chain fluid.

7. Replenish the primary-case oil if the level does not reach the outer diameter of the diaphragm clutch spring. Use Harley's gear-case oil—the major H-D wrenches prefer it.

8. Install the new derby cover, paying particular attention to its flatness

1. Use care removing and reinstalling the derby hardware, it's not all that robust because it doesn't need to be. Leave the breaker bar in the toolbox for this task.

2. Beneath the cover is the clutch on both the Big Twin and Sportster models. The primary fluid level is supposed to be even with the outer edge of the clutch basket.

around the mating flange and to the clocking of the bolt holes. If anything fails to line up, take the part back to your dealer and get a new one. The three bolts are equidistant around the circumference, so, save for any graphics on the front of the derby cover, it doesn't matter which face is up.

9. Install the retaining screws—either the stockers or any special fasteners that may have come with the new cover, remembering to use the stock H-D grommetted washers—and torque them to the value the cover manufacturer recommends. Failing specific instructions, torque the bolts to 120 to 130 inch-pounds.

10. Run the bike and check for leaks.

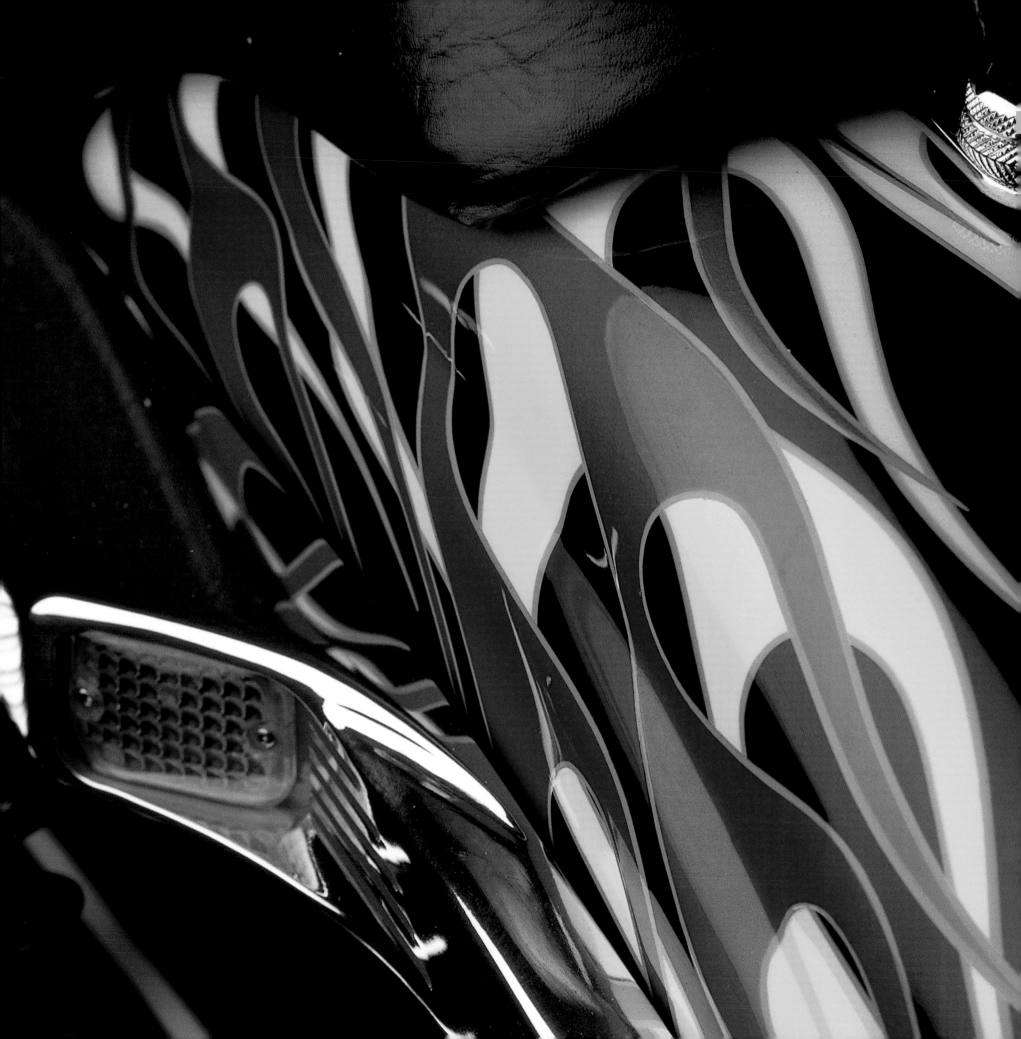

Chapter 2:

Paint: A New Skin

A good repaint will be the centerpiece of your rolling artwork, an in-your-face presentation of what you and your painter think is the coolest thing in pigments.

As Harley rolls into its 95th anniversary, paint is a high priority—both for Harley as a manufacturer and for the owners as a means of customization. And even though what was true in the teens—that your typical Harley is a simple device, without acres of bodywork and unnecessary plumage—remains true today, it is nonetheless accurate to say that its assortment of metal and plastic is still a canvas of considerable size and varying dimensions for personal expression. Taking an otherwise stock bike and merely re-

painting the tank, covers, and fenders will result in a stunning alteration to the overall look.

But going with a new paint job isn't a risk-free, surefire endeavor. For one thing, once you've started down the road to custom paint, you can't go back. If your goal was to keep your bike in the condition that will maximize resale value, it's probably not a good idea to let your imagination run wild with the painter's gun.

There are exceptions, of course, particularly if you stick with a conservative scheme that is somewhat like, but not an exact duplicate of, a Harley paint job. A radical paint rework that embodies everything you want in a finish may not agree with all tastes. As Jon Kosmoski, founder of House of Kolor, the preeminent supplier of paint to the custom world, emphasizes, "Beauty really is in the eye of the beholder. A painter has to have compatible ideas with the customer." Keep that in mind.

Opposite: Overlapping the colors of the flames requires different coats of paint applied sequentially. This, naturally, calls for masking first one color and then the next. Clearcoating after the final layer of flames, and then sanding the whole surface down flush, makes for a professional job.

Above: Here's a custom trick that should not be overlooked: continuing the paint theme through other parts of the bike, like the air-cleaner cover and the oil tank. Note also the juxtaposition of the checkered-flag motif with the customary flames.

Left: Pinstriping is done with fine brushes and loads of patience. Savvy painters will have a shoeboxful of brushes, some trimmed to within a hair of their lives, to paint exactly the thickness of line wanted. It takes a steady hand.

Above: An otherwise stock Road King receives a coat of pearl white over the standard blue single exterior color. It's a stock-looking scheme that will dazzle those who know that Harley never made one this way.

Let's consider the positive side, then: A good repaint will be the centerpiece of your rolling artwork, an in-your-face presentation of what you and your painter think is the coolest thing in pigments. It's perhaps your best opportunity to say, "This bike is *mine.*"

How to Do It

In order to know what to ask a prospective painter, it helps to understand the basic process of painting Harley bodywork.

At this point—assuming that the underlying bodywork is undamaged—you're faced with a dilemma. Do you take the paint all the way down to metal, or do you allow the painter to start from the factory primer? Some shops start a paint job by sanding or stripping down to below the level of Harley's insignia, which is usually applied just below the clearcoat. Other shops insist on going down to the factory primer. "You can start with the factory Harley primer on a newer bike if it's in good condition," says Kosmoski. "But for parts where you don't know the quality of the primer—someone else's paint job, a preprimed aftermarket part—you really need to go all the way to the metal."

In the large view, going with a strip-to-primer job for a simple, economical paint job isn't such a bad thing. It's when you opt for the all-bells, all-whistles type of repaint—particularly in schemes with a lot of different layers of color and pinstriping—that you want the best possible base.

Other painters disagree on this point. "You wouldn't build a new house over an old foundation," says Ron Morelli, of Ron's Custom Paint in Hayward, California. "And I will not start even a simple paint job without going right to the metal and applying new primer." Ultimately, you'll end up letting the individual painter be your guide, because his familiarity with the various and significantly different painting methods and chemicals will set his comfort level.

Opposite: This Heritage Softail's base paint is stock. By sanding down through the decals and overlaying ghosted flames, the appearance changes dramatically. Note also the chrome lifter bodies and oil pump, as well as the Arlen Ness floorboards.

Above: Flame paint schemes are the customizer's touchstone. This is a classic red-and-orange flame job with light blue outline. Notice also how the flame theme is carried through the speedometer face.

Right: Classic Harley colors are an almost surefire way to have a custom paint job that will appeal to a broad range of riders. This is an important consideration if you plan to sell the bike eventually.

It should be no surprise that the first part of the paint job, priming, is one of the most critical. A primer does several things. First, it acts as a sealer and corrosion inhibitor; as such, it needs to bond with the material it's used against. Epoxy primers, used almost universally these days, have superior adhesion qualities compared with the single-part primers of yesteryear. A good primer will ensure that any body filler stays below the primer layer. There's nothing worse than having the filler leach through, because it changes the texture and color of the final coat.

In addition, the primer acts as an anchor for the paint job, giving the paint a nice, chemically "grippy" surface. Ever seen paint flake off something and leave the primer behind? This is an example of incompatible materials or poor prep work.

Primers come in several flavors. Some are purely for sealing the panel, while others have high solids content—meaning they're thicker

1. Pro painter Ron Morelli uses thin masking tape and studied moves to trace the design's shape. He may try several times to trace the flames to his satisfaction. This is an art form that cannot be rushed.

2. Illustrative paint work requires extensive preparation and a skilled airbrush artist for successful results. Because these schemes have several paint layers, they can be fragile and difficult to keep looking new. Note the siren-style air cleaner from Custom Chrome.

Opposite: Screaming yellow paint jobs—as on this White Brothers rolling showroom—are definitely for extroverts. Use of a single color on frame, body panels, seat, and headlight nacelle is a bold way of tying together the shapes of the motorcycle.

Below: A reworked instrument nacelle makes for a smoother integration of the tach and speedo. Some customizers use fiberglass for this type of modification, while others prefer the harder (yet more rewarding) method of bending, shaping, and welding metal.

than other primers—to aid in removing small surface blemishes. These are called primer-surfacers. Look for a painter who uses a primer-sealer coat before the paint.

Priming the Parts

Assuming you're dealing with a shooter who will take your parts down to the bare material, his first step before applying primer will be to carefully clean and dry the parts. If there's any bodywork to be performed, it will be done before the first primer coat. Try to ascertain through your visits with the painter how this bodywork will be done. You want to avoid as much plastic body filler as you can. Even the best filler can crack out over time. The tried-and-true metalworking methods of dent removal are by far the best, although use of a small amount of body filler won't dramatically compromise the job.

Next, any basic masking will be performed. Insist that your painter mask off the fuel-tank opening, the petcock threads, oil-tank hose fittings, and close-tolerance items like motor mount plates. Any paint left open to liquids like fuel or oil will eventually allow the fluids under the paint by capillary action. The fuel filler opening, for example, should be masked off along the upper surface of the tank, not down in the filler cavity. You also don't want the multiple coats of paint to interfere dimensionally with the fit of the engine, transmission, or suspension components. Any part with metal-to-metal contact will eventually wear away the paint, possibly chipping out into a cosmetically critical area.

Jon Kosmoski's House of Kolor

Kosmoski started House of Color in 1959 as a body shop. In time, Kosmoski discovered that some of the available paints limited his artistic expression, so he began experimenting with different paint mixtures and techniques. By 1965, Kosmoski began manufacturing and selling his own line of paint; and while the original body shop was named "House of Color," the George Barris influence took hold and the paint line became House of Kolor.

If Kosmoski has a calling card in the custom car and bike field, it's his extensive experience with outrageous colors and textures. Much of Kosmoski's knowledge was gained the hard way. "I made a lot of mistakes and tried a lot of things that didn't work," Kosmoski says. "And, in the early years, I was not about to let my secrets out. If somebody asked how I did something, I wouldn't tell them. Many of the other painters of the time [the early 1960s] would flat-out lie about techniques."

Today, House of Kolor is practically revered in the custom-painting circles. This is in part because of the enormous selection of colors and full systems; these incorporate compatible epoxy primers, base coats, candy or pearl clearcoats, and plain clearcoats. Moreover, House of Kolor provides a full line of noncatalyzed illustration paint.

What is perhaps the greatest asset to the painter in the street is House of Kolor's extensive technical library. Take the time, and you can learn more than you ever imagined about the House of Kolor line and how to apply it. The firm also has instructional videotapes and a paint chip chart with more than 600 different hues.

The overall effect of a colorful paint job is to dramatize the lines of the bike. This Softail has a stock-shape tank and bobbed rear fender, but the uncommon paint scheme renders this bike quite apart from your off-the-shelf Softail.

Generally, after the first primer coat, a second primer coat will be applied and allowed to cure overnight. It's vitally important that the painter does not rush the primer steps; if you apply a finish coat too soon and the solvents in the primer do not have enough time to flash out, they'll be trapped under the paint, which only means they'll take longer to get to the surface. Rest assured, get to the surface they will.

Then the pro painter will shoot a guide coat of a dark color before the first base coat—this helps to make sure all the bodywork has been done properly. By cross-sanding through the dark guide coat, the painter can easily see the high and low spots in the surfaces. These should be knocked completely smooth before the next step. If he's in doubt that all the imperfections have been sanded smooth, the painter may apply additional layers of guide coat. Some painters use a dark primer/surfacer in lieu of a traditional guide coat, so this layer may or may not have to be sanded completely away before continuing.

Another sanding takes place the next morning with about 400-grit sandpaper and soapy water, and any touch-ups are made as necessary, followed by a sealer coat. Then the base color coat goes on, followed in twenty minutes by a clearcoat. Typically, a quality custom job will call for four coats of base and clear, applied at about twenty-minute intervals. The paint is allowed to cure overnight and is sanded the next day with 1500-grit sandpaper.

Above: **Subtle pinstriping can work wonders for an otherwise plain bagger. It's clean and tidy, yet clearly sets itself apart from showroom-stock counterparts.**

Opposite: Just because it's a touring bike doesn't mean flames are out of place on a bagger. Many riders like the juxtaposition of sedate bodywork—saddlebags even—and a wild paint scheme. This bike is also quite stout of engine, with an S&S carburetor, Thunderheader pipe, and high-lift camshaft. It's perhaps not your typical interstate trawler.

Right: Notice how the split line for the tank is perfectly matched to a new sheet-metal cover atop the upper frame tubes on this FXR. It makes it possible to remove the tank, yet maintains a smooth, almost unbroken line from steering head to taillight. This is true artisanship.

If you've chosen a two-tone scheme, the second color would be applied over the base coat after proper and time-consuming masking and sanding of the area. Three coats of the second color are usually applied, in the same sequence as the base coats. The last application of clearcoat will be allowed to sit overnight and the whole piece sanded with 1500-grit paper and subsequently polished with a low-speed buffing machine. Insignia go on below two or more additional layers of clearcoat.

Of course, you can opt for something more exotic than your basic two-tone glossy job; there are metallic, candy, and pearl finishes to be had as well.

Heavy Metal, Candy, and Pearl Jam for Your Baby

A metallic is simply standard glossy paint with aluminum flakes mixed in; there are many levels of fineness in the metal flake.

A candy finish includes a basic glossy base coat with a series of transparent top color coats that change the overall perception of the color. It is the effect that seems to make the paint fist-deep.

A pearl finish uses a similar philosophy to create a very different effect. Pearl is itself a composite medium of mica and a substrate that comes in a powder or slurry and is mixed into the clearcoat.

It is optically transparent when viewed directly, but changes into reflectivity (in the color of the top coat, à la candy) as the finish is viewed at an angle.

House of Kolor has recently introduced a base "Kandy" coat that allows the candy look without requiring as many coats. On that topic, Kosmoski says, "A lot of guys think that the more paint the better. That's not true. You want to get the job done in no more than 6- to 8-mil thickness." Thicker paint tends to be much more brittle, so any flexing of painted parts can lead to cracking or "spider-webbing" of the finish.

Picking Your Paint

While some painters are comfortable working with any paints, most seem to prefer certain brands, and many choose House of Kolor paints. In any case, make sure your painter is comfortable with the materials; don't insist on PPG or Du Pont to a hard-core House of Kolor man.

And while a few painters still use older enamels, you will be better served by using a more modern, epoxy-based paint. Why? The newest types—there's a lot of research and development going on in paint, incidentally—are worlds ahead of the old standbys. They're more flexible, less prone to degradation by ultraviolet radiation, and much easier to keep looking glossy.

Finally, when you get your newly painted pieces back, check carefully for scratches, chips, runs, drips, and any other blemishes. An expensive paint job should be nearly perfect. A conscientious shop should, within reason, gladly rework anything you don't like.

Consider some other aspects of the job: How does the shop finish the undersides of the parts? The top-flight firms will apply a thin layer of undercoating to the bottoms of fenders to prevent rock dings from damaging the paint and possibly creating a chip on the outside of the part. At the very least, you shouldn't see evidence of overspray or careless application of paint. Don't settle for the line: "Ah...you'll never see that." With a big-buck job, the work on the places you don't normally see is part of what you're paying for.

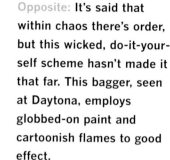

Opposite: It's said that within chaos there's order, but this wicked, do-it-yourself scheme hasn't made it that far. This bagger, seen at Daytona, employs globbed-on paint and cartoonish flames to good effect.

Above: This Sportster's candy purple, single-color coat was applied by the owner, a first-time painter. It has no badges, adornment, or pinstriping. The single color is highlighted by generous chroming of the stock engine cases, belt guards, and oil tank. Note also the chrome Kury Akyn Hypercharger air cleaner and chrome rear master cylinder cover.

Harley's Color Shop

No doubt a lot of riders are apprehensive about venturing into a painter's shop and handing over expensive pieces of a motorcycle. So it is with this owner in mind that Harley has created its custom paint program. Basically a list of new-production bodywork pieces that are painted in custom colors, many of them carefully color-matched with accessories, custom paints can be bought through your Harley dealer.

Harley has the system set up in two tiers. First is the bodywork sets. When you plop down the dough for a Color Shop redo, you get all-new fenders, tank, and, when appropriate, oil tank. Harley has at least one set of custom color schemes for each bike family and usually two or three schemes. Generally, these schemes have simplified graphics or an even more classic look than the stock scheme. The Color Shop treatment also applies to Road King saddlebags.

The second tier includes a slew of color-matched components like air-cleaner covers, oil tanks, battery covers, belt guards, fender rails, instrument nacelles, and other details. Again, you are buying new, standard-production Harley parts painted in one of about seven hues. This is a handy program for those who want to highlight the standard bike's paint scheme without having to remove and repaint the original components.

That same benefit is also the program's biggest drawback to many riders. You pay for duplicate bodywork when you can only use one set at a time. (Boosters of the Color Shop theme say you can change your bike to suit your mood, but it's no half-hour affair to pull fenders and tanks.)

Finally, remember that the Color Shop items go through the regular Harley painting process, which means that the quality is generally quite good, but not up to the standards of a truly custom job. The insignia will not be dropped way down into the paint, as a genuine pro shooter would insist on as a matter of course. And with just a few color schemes in any given year, there's no guarantee you won't pass your twin going the other way down the A1A in Daytona.

As part of the Harley Color Shop, this kit for the 1997-and-later Sportsters uses a gray and burnt orange scheme. With the Color Shop kits, you get all-new bodywork—in this case, fuel tank and fenders—with pinstriping and logos in place. This is a truly bolt-on paint job that, for about $1000, still leaves you with your stock parts.

For Dyna Glide models—except the Dyna Wide Glide—Harley's Color Shop offers this teal scheme. It's more expensive than the Sporty kit because there's more to it: tank, fenders, fender rails, rocker-box inserts, air-cleaner cover, battery box, and coil cover (not shown; it's on the left side of the bike).

1. Monochrome Gray is the theme for Heritage Classics or Fat Boys. This more comprehensive Softail kit includes the fenders, fender rails, fuel tank, oil tank, instrument nacelle, and rocker-box inserts.

2. Not only are the Color Shop components available in whole kits, they can be purchased separately. This collection for the Sportsters includes air-cleaner cover, oil tank, battery side and top covers, left-side electrical cover, belt guard, and fender rails. Eight colors are available for the XL parts. Other components available for the entire line include the round air-cleaner cover, horn covers, Big Twin derby and timing covers, and rocker-box inserts.

3. For Road King models, Harley's Color Shop has this Birch White and Scarlet Red two-tone set that includes fenders, fuel tank, and side covers. Separately, new fiberglass saddlebags, in the two-tone or a single Birch White scheme, are available.

4. Another Dyna Color Shop offering is this High Impact Blue kit. Almost everything that's painted on the bike is replaced with new hardware in the kit.

5. For Softail models, the Color Shop components include the oil tank, fender rails, and instrument nacelle in black, Lazer Red Pearl, Midnight Red, Patriot Red Pearl, Sinister Blue Pearl, States Blue, Victory Red Sun Glo, and Violet Pearl.

6. Components for the Dyna Glide models include fender rails, upper belt guard, battery side and top covers, and coil cover in black, Lazer Red Pearl, Patriot Red Pearl, States Blue, and Violet Pearl.

7. Think back to 1965. For Heritage Classic models, the Color Shop has this Mint Green and black color combination. You get new fenders and fuel tank with this kit.

Other Considerations

That covers the basics of what will happen to your beloved Harley parts. Now it's time to consider what exactly you're going to have done.

Other multicolored graphic treatments may recall some significant model in Harley's storied past—the ever popular 1950s Electrolux tints against a cream base is an enduring favorite. Or you may want to reproduce the orange-and-black Harley racing livery. You'll find no shortage of Sportsters painted up to look like XR750 dirt trackers that turned right instead of left at the end of the front straight. Nothing wrong with celebrating Harley's competition dominance, that's for sure.

Cast your glance further afield and you will find those ultra customs done in comprehensive monochromatic schemes that tie everything from the tank to the master cylinder into a single color— here the mechanical bits of the engine, in chrome or black, work with the seat and tires to form the few elements of contrast. Some of these schemes may have a single, intentionally jarring, dissimilar color to break the pattern. (Bear in mind that the true pros in the field aim for a distinctive style. Says Kosmoski, "I will never copy another painter's work, color for color. That doesn't mean you won't find guys borrowing good ideas, but the top painters won't copy.")

Opposite: **Black is by far the favorite custom color in the Harley world. You can see why. It's so basic and elemental, and it allows the chrome and polish of the engine and chassis to stand out. Note also the Custom Chrome mirrors and Jay Brake O-ring handgrips.**

Left: **The gracefulness of the flames on the typically rounded Fat Bob tank contrasts with the gleaming angularity of the Ness air cleaner and rocker boxes.**

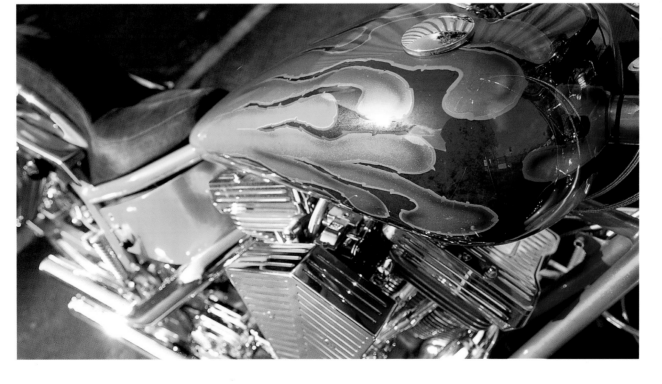

Rory of Rory's Creations does everything freehand, even designs that are to duplicate an existing style. Other painters may use stencils or even decals, but in the rarefied air of the painter-artists, only hand-drawn designs will do.

You must also consider how to implement any graphics like the Harley logo, the model, or some other bit of bike-side billboardism. Care to trumpet the fact that you're riding a genuine H-D? Prefer to recall old corporate logos? Maybe you would just prefer to state your name, rank, and serial number along the sides of your machine. No matter—there's no shortage of skilled illustrators who will toil alongside the primary painter to offer the ultimate in custom work.

Whatever scheme you choose or color combination you pick, one thing is certain: A quality job will reward you time and again, while a quick-and-dirty job invites frustration and heartache. If you're thinking you can save a few bones on the paint job, stop right here. Customizers will tell you—it's just not worth it. For that reason, among many, you need to choose your shooter carefully.

Choosing the Right Painter

To find a quality painter in your area, start by looking at your local Harley dealer or wherever the Milwaukee iron gathers. It won't take long for you to spy an out-of-the-ordinary paint job; and because most bike owners with custom paint are proud of the fact, it's likely they'll be glad to tell you who did the work.

Then take the time to visit the painter-in-question's shop. It should look more like a factory than a garage sale run amok. Keep an eye out for a clean spray booth and paint guns that aren't caked over in old paint. Painting is a messy

"While there are many back-alley Michelangelos around, steer clear of the fellow who paints as a sideline to, say, working at the post office."

1. Ghosting of flames is done by painting the secondary and tertiary layers in colors similar to the base coat's. Creating depth in a paint job often requires several coats, but much of the luminance comes from using gradated paint colors or solids in the paint to provide reflection of ambient light.

2. A basic dark purple-flames paint job is set off by the gleaming chrome Arlen Ness tank panel and fuel-filler caps.

business, but the real pros will want a work area that's as clean as they can make it.

And, while there are surely many back-alley Michelangelos around, steer clear of the fellow who paints as a sideline to, say, working at the post office. A competent, serious painter has a reputation to nurture and preserve and is less likely to risk a shoddy job for the occasional quick buck. You don't have the same assurances from the shadetree shooter. Similarly, you would be well served to pick a painter who does much of his work on bikes. Admittedly, you'll find a lot of talent in the auto-painting field—particularly those businesses that specialize in top-end exotics—but there are myriad tricks of the trade in dealing with motorcycle parts that push the odds in favor of the dedicated bike shooter. For example, does the shop have fixtures for holding bike parts? "I made all my own fixtures,"

Kosmoski says. "I've seen shops with tanks hanging from the roof of the paint booth, but I don't like painting dancing parts."

You should expect the painter to be forthcoming about all costs involved in the project. Because many paint shops are small businesses with cyclic cash flow, it has become common to ask for some part of the payment in advance. Some shops will ask for half, while others will require some portion to help offset the cost of the raw materials. Be suspicious of the painter who wants all the money upfront. It helps to have some leverage to make sure the quality of the work is equal to what you're paying.

In addition, the painter should be able to give you a close estimate of the time he'll need. There's nothing worse than planning a vacation right after a major bike rework only to have the painter fail to meet your time line because he (or the chromer

Right: Contrasting scallops are another favorite of the custom painter. The juxtaposition of the colors is a popular custom-car trick. Notice the custom handlebar clamp. These are often more for show than for real-world utility.

Below: Cloud-like detailing is done in one of several ways, including the age-old method of dabbing the still-wet base coat with wadded-up nylons or plastic wrap. Note that the paint scheme is repeated on the steering head and forward frame tubes.

surfacers, are quite expensive. They are, almost without exception, worth the cost.

With the aforementioned variations of scheme in mind—which should in the large view mesh with your own color-wheel research—you should have the basic scheme for your bike in mind. Know what you want before you start.

This is particularly important, because once you're faced with the dazzling array of colors, and the exponentially greater combinations thereof, it's easy to just glaze over in awe.

You should plan to spend a few hours mulling over the schemes and colors with your hired gun. This is where your investment in time with the prospective painter will reap great dividends. Painters at high-profile shops will sit down with the customer and discuss the scheme and colors in great detail. The range of colors, for example, can seem staggering; from the straightforward glossies to pearls to candies to metallics, the virtually infinite combinations of colors and textures can make 31 Flavors seem like mere chocolate and vanilla. Specify your color choice by its paint number as well as by name to avoid potential confusion. Paints with similar-sounding names can be vastly different.

By far the most useful implement on the painter's tool belt is a photo album of past work. You get some sense of the possibilities and might find a color and scheme up to that point visible only to the mind's eye. Morelli says, "I will sit down with a customer and pore over the photos for

1. Generally, the more garish the scheme, the louder the colors. Look closely to see the contrasting blue or purple outlines on the flames; this is essential to make them stand out from the background. Note also the collection of Ron Sims lightning-bolt accessories: derby and points covers, transmission end cap, air-cleaner insert, footpegs, floorboards, and nut covers.

2. So-called taildragger fenders help accentuate a bike's lowness, as well as the owner's desire to stand out from the crowd. To look right, such a fender will require a larger rear tire—which in turn calls for an offset belt drive and, possibly, frame modification.

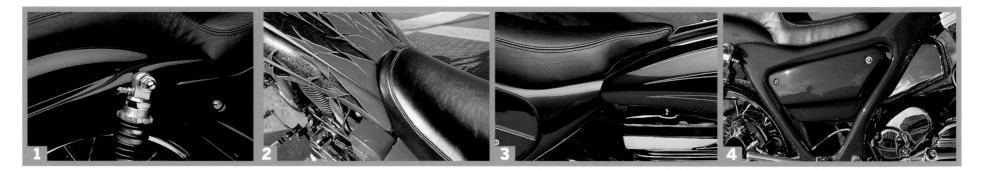

1. **Upper frame rails are wrapped in steel sheet on this FXR to create a smooth transition from the gas tank.**

2. **Clever metalwork here "stretches" the tank to mate more closely with the side covers and seat. This is not a simple procedure, so it's best left to the professionals. Many ready-made stretched tanks are available, though.**

3. **A stretched gas tank and custom-fabricated panels around the side-panel area make for a smooth, uncluttered look.**

4. **Here, the FXR's frame rails have been molded. This involves smoothing the welds and either welding in new steel pieces or filling in the voids with body filler, which you can see on the frame tubes below the side cover. For larger spans, such as the sections above the cover, the new-sheet-metal method is preferred. Body filler can fill only smaller gaps without the risk of cracking over time.**

an hour or more. I want to make sure we both have a solid idea of what he wants."

Reviewing a photo documentary of the painter's past "canvases" will also give you some inkling of the quality of his work and the types of designs he specializes in. Take note of the style of the creations—if you're hot for flames but the craftsman in question has accomplished few such projects, consider finding a painter with more flames experience.

Other Custom Tricks

The long-standing customizers don't stop at a trick paint job. There are other detail jobs that can really bring a custom bike together.

One is something called finger sanding or frame dressing. It's a straightforward idea that needs to be meticulously implemented to be successful over the long run. The object is to remove the unsightly welds that are part of every stock Harley frame—and the aftermarket frames, too.

The body man carefully grinds down the outermost layer of the weld, paying particular attention to not reduce the strength of the frame or

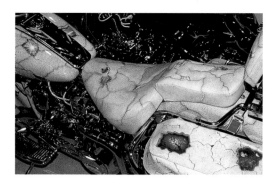

Left: **Airbrushing is an art form popular with custom Harley painters. Here a bagger gets an overall sandstone look with "broken out" vignettes.**

compromise the weld itself. Once smoothed, the joint receives a layer of flexible body filler, which is allowed to cure fully. Then comes the tedious process of sanding the filler to produce a smooth, seamless fillet from frame tube to frame tube. It's crucial that the body man has had good success with his techniques in this area—try to find a frame that was molded a few years ago and see how it's held up.

Engine Painting

Because the bodywork is just part of the overall appearance package, it's common for full-on customs to have outlandish paint applied to the engine. A few caveats apply here: Make sure that any paint used will tolerate reasonably high temperatures; the last thing you want is to have the paint begin to chip and flake off the cylinder fins after a few heat-and-cool cycles. (Ultimately, you may have to settle for some discoloration around the exhaust port, due to the high temperatures there. Not all paints and colors tolerate heat equally well.)

Further, be sure that any mating surfaces are properly masked and protected. Paint the case parting line or the lifter block surfaces, for example, and you'll have oil leaks you'll never fix, no matter how extreme the magic cure. For a good seal, the gaskets must be touching bare metal, not some painted surface.

Above: **Fairing the taillight into the fender is commonly called "frenching." It's most often done with fiberglass and body filler, but a few hardy metal pounders will create the shapes needed to surround the taillight from welded steel. This bike also has custom-made fender rails and a Bartels' exhaust system.**

Right: **Trim details on the FL's tank carry through the basic shape of the instrument panel, which has been accented with a Harley's Parts & Accessories bezel insert.**

Chapter 3:

Seats: A Rear View

Many new-Harley owners have a replacement saddle in mind well before the dealer's prep department has finished filling the bike's battery.

The seat is one of the main elements in your Harley's ergonomic package and is high on the totem pole of items that determine your bike's comfort. A thin slab of leather that barely keeps you off the frame rails may well be tolerable for a short afternoon drive—and it certainly looks great—but if you have more demanding duties in mind, forget it. After the first fuel stop, you'll be ready to call for a cab *and* a chiropractor.

It shouldn't be hard to make a comfortable, attractive seat, right?

Take a Seat

Unfortunately, the backside is not only one of the more sensitive parts of our bodies, but it is one with tremendous variation in tolerances—preference, if you will—from person to person. Differ-

ent riders will have vastly different takes on what constitutes the ultimate saddle. Mix in that monkey-wrench-wielding variable called *style*, and you can see why the aftermarket is practically awash in foam, vinyl, and leather.

All these reasons probably explain why many new-Harley owners have a replacement saddle in mind well before the dealer's prep department has finished filling the bike's battery. Admittedly, for some riders the standard seat is just fine, thanks very much. But for others, the stock saddle is just not what they're looking for.

Walk the line at any Harley gathering and you'll see that most riders have decided, for reasons of form or function, to utter a derivative of an Arlen Ness mantra: "No stock seats." It's not hard to find a saddle to stand in for the stocker, either. So it

Above: **Harley's Badlander vinyl seat takes advantage of low frame rails and thin construction to provide a low seat height. It needs to have firmer padding to make this stance possible without compromising comfort.**

Left: **A custom leather seat by Stitcher on this Bartels'-built bike follows traditional chopper styling cues.**

Opposite: **This Corbin leather solo seat mimics the stock Harley seat's basic outline but uses Corbin's typically stiff foam and leather envelope.**

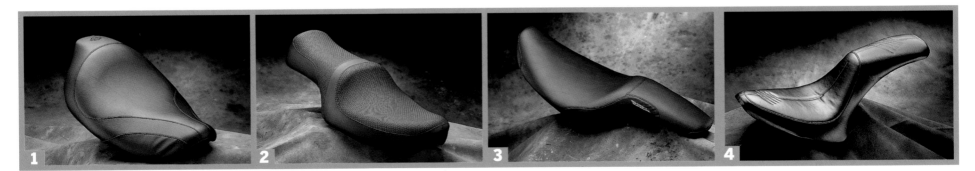

1. As part of Harley's Diamondback collection, this solo saddle must be used with matching tail sections.

2. Basket-weave facing is a hallmark of Harley's Sportster Sport vinyl saddle; it is also available as a replacement for other XL models.

3. This Badlander model from Harley has a slightly less pronounced step.

4. Le Pera also makes more outlandish designs, like this one with a stitched accent and cursory passenger portion. Many of these ultracustom seats are intended for urban riding, and passengers aren't expected to sit on them for very long.

seems that replacement seats exist for every Harley made today and the vast majority of erstwhile models. Prices range from a budget-watcher $150 to an astounding $3,000 for a virtually one-of-a-kind work of perchable art.

Harley's Way

It's part of Harley's predicament as a manufacturer to accomplish several goals with regard to seats: Appeal to a broad range of riders and tastes (even in the same motorcycle), pass some strict in-house guidelines for suitability and durability, and trim costs wherever possible. What may be surprising is the lengths to which Harley goes in concocting a seat for a new model. Such efforts are largely because the call from riders, much to the consternation of those charged with making the seats, is overwhelmingly for a riding position close to the ground. According to one Harley source, low seat height is the main demand of the consumer.

Generally, the seat department gets ahold of a new model well into the development phase, so the seat maker's call for lower frame rails often gets thrown into the hopper for the next model revi-

sion. But those alterations eventually come along. Harley took the opportunity with the 1997 FL models to reconfigure some of the underseat real estate to make it possible to both lower the seat rails and fit the saddle closer to the rails. This results in a lower seat height without having to mercilessly hack foam out of the seat.

Harley's in-house designers have a great advantage over the aftermarket types because each new model is presented not only to the normal-production staff, but to the designers in the Genuine Motor Accessories division. So with any major changes to a model, the Milwaukee staff gets a serious leg up, if you will, on the guys looking through the factory gate from the outside.

But Harley's designers also have to walk the middle ground. Even if a model's styling elements call for a radical low, thin seat, the internal dictates of function and broad-based appeal often step in and call for a different, moderate tack. And some truly wild expressions of butt-bumper art may never get beyond the drawing board for the same broad-appeal reasons. (That does not, however, hinder the aftermarket.)

On the motorcycle, the flow of the
Diamondback set is evident. A tank panel
and tail section bracket the Diamondback solo
saddle. Note that you cannot use the
solo saddle without the tailpiece.

1. **Le Pera's LN-545 basket-weave vinyl saddle balances good looks with passenger comfort.**

2. **Danny Gray's Mini Tour seat is made from leather. Gray is Arlen Ness's seat maker of choice and sells through the Ness catalog.**

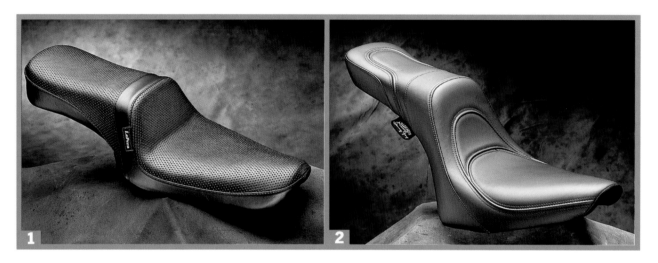

What's Important in a Seat?

Let's face facts: The motorcycle saddle exists to give you someplace to sit. Unlike automobiles, the motorcycle has limited real estate for this task. Makers of touring motorcycles, which are intended to be used for all-day stints, spend considerable effort designing and building a comfortable seat. Getting just the right perch isn't as easy as throwing some foam and leather over the seat rails and calling it a day.

To determine how to build a seat—from the point of view of Harley or the aftermarketers—you have to first determine the motorcycle's mission. Is your bike the two-wheeled equivalent of a street rod—a bar-hopping, looks-are-everything rolling sculpture? Do you intend to use your bike for commuting? How about long-distance travel?

Each of these categories imposes vastly different requirements on the seats and creates headaches of varying intensities for the seat designers. Seat comfort is dependent on several variables, including seat shape and foam density, rider weight, seating position, length of ride, and, of course, the highly changeable human tolerances for weight distribution.

As a rule, the seat that best distributes your weight over as large an area as you can stand—and this is, obviously, different for each individual—will be the most comfortable. Some riders prefer slimmer saddles that don't push their legs outward at a stop sign, while others like a broad, flat perch that allows for some moving-around room on those long hauls. Seat makers are not universal in their beliefs, either. Mike Corbin, arguably the premier aftermarket-seat guru, prefers to have a slightly crowned shape to most of his designs; he argues that the bottom of a human is not shaped like the bottom of a picnic table. Other makers take

"Getting just the right perch isn't as easy as throwing some foam and leather over the seat rails and calling it a day."

slightly different approaches to the seat shape, and you might find that theirs are more comfortable in the long run than the crowned model. Unfortunately, there's almost no way of knowing for sure until you have some miles in the saddle.

Something else to keep in mind concerns the remainder of your bike's ergonomic package. Think about how much of your weight must be carried by the seat. Do you have footpegs right under your seat and a drag bar? For bikes with more rear-set footpegs and shorter or drag-style bars, like Dyna Glides, FXRs, and Sportsters, the rider's buttocks aren't handling most of his weight. Other models, in contrast, with forward-set footpegs and pullback handlebars often place a great deal of the rider's weight on the backside. In between, you have bikes with floorboards and moderate handlebar bends. Each calls for a slightly different kind of seat.

As Mike Corbin points out, "You have to consider the ergonomics carefully. A feet-forward riding position not only puts more weight on the buttocks, but it stretches out the muscles in the backside. For this type of bike, you have to spread out the load and support it with high-density foam." Indeed, Corbin's saddles have long held the reputation for being just a bit more cushy than a two-by-four. So, apehanger fans, shop carefully and ask around for recommendations from fellow riders. (Many riders of this type of bike just up and admit that riding all day isn't what this motorcycle thing is all about. Decide early on if this is your tack.)

Figuring Foam

If the seat cover is the face of a saddle, then the foam padding inside is as surely the critical skeleton. And like a med-school anatomy model assembled without instructions, it's easy to get it wrong.

According to the seat manufacturers, by far the sin most often committed is to fit seats with too-soft foam. Many believe that the initial showroom impression is responsible for this. A buyer walks into the dealership and sits on several different models; he does so for only a minute at a time. Often,

Corbin's leather pad for the Storz Performance dirttrack look-alike mimics the functionality of racing perches. It's firm and fairly square-edged, so you probably wouldn't want to put in too many 500-mile days on it.

the softer seat will feel more comfortable for that short-term experience. He may think it will be the better saddle for the long run.

Not so. Here's what happens: After only a few miles, that soft foam will pack down under his weight, leaving this hapless rider's backside resting on the unyielding seat base. And because the average Harley seat is made to fit as closely as possible to the seat rails and underpinnings, there's little likelihood that the seat pan will be smooth and comfortable. Predictably, by the end of the first long afternoon, our new rider has a serious case of numb-butt.

If, with moderate effort, you can poke your thumb right through a seat's padding and come up against the seat base, it's probably too soft.

Harley and most of the aftermarket manufacturers use a two-part liquid urethane foam that combines and expands inside a mold. By altering the chemical makeup of the parts, a seat maker can create finished foams of just about any firmness. The difference is in the size and quantity of air bubbles or voids in the foam; the more voids, the softer the foam will feel. It's important during manufacture to ensure that the poured foam expands into the molds without creating large, unintended voids.

A few aftermarket builders use sheet foam cut and trimmed to size. This is done mainly because it's less expensive for low-volume constructors to make seats this way; the foam-mixing machines and molds are expensive, and costs must be amortized over a fairly hefty production run for the two-part method to make business sense. Properly done, there's little difference in the final product. (You shouldn't, however, feel any voids under the seat cover in a cut-foam saddle.)

For either foam source, though, there's usually some hand trimming required to make the padding fit the base and cover.

1. Mustang's studded Softail seat is made from durable vinyl. Proponents of vinyl over leather point to its greater longevity—particularly when the bike is parked outside for any length of time—as a key feature.

2. A touring saddle needs greater surface area for daylong comfort; this Mustang saddle is obviously intended for the long haul.

Left: Another Le Pera Silhouette vinyl saddle; notice how its shape follows the outline of the fender rail.

In any well-designed seat, the precise density of the foam will vary according to the intended use of the seat and bike. A large touring rig, for example, will more often than not have thick, somewhat soft foam. Sportier models will utilize firm foam in less quantity, and the style-is-the-word offerings sometimes have to resort to park-bench-stiff stuffing to accommodate a razor-like profile and still have some utility.

Base of It All

Like most volume manufacturers, Harley aims to cut production costs and speed delivery time. For this reason, Harley's seat bases are for the most part injection-molded polyethylene plastic. Most aftermarket manufacturers don't employ this material because the tooling costs are prohibitive and the spool-up time can be greater than for steel or fiberglass bases. Many aftermarketers claim the plastic seat bases are too flexible and distort once a heavy rider hops aboard.

Corbin uses bases made from chopped fiberglass and molded integrally with the foam padding. Others, like Le Pera and Mustang, opt for stamped-steel bases. Still others, like Danny Gray, Drag Specialties, and Saddlemen, use ABS plastic bases molded much like the OEM version.

Le Pera, in particular, takes great pride in the metal seat base; it fits the powdercoated part with a protective layer of carpet and vinyl edging to prevent cutting through the top cover. Le Pera makes its own dies from custom-stamped bases whose rivet holes are prestamped. All mounting tangs are welded in place, one of the

1. Corbin's Hollywood Solo for the Softail is normally made of leather, and there are several optional skins, like this ostrich.

2. Corbin's Fast Gunfighter is a tight-fitting semisolo saddle that is intended for looks rather than touring-style comfort. It is a more accommodating saddle than most cruiser pads because it has a decent layer of foam.

3. Corbin Gunfighter and Lady is an older but still extremely popular design made in leather. A generous passenger pad combines with a pronounced lip at the rear for a high spouse-comfort factor.

4. Corbin's leather Gunfighter is also available for the older FXR bikes.

great advantages of a steel base pad. Mustang makes its base plates similarly.

What's important to keep in mind here is that while each type of seat base has its inherent advantages, it's the quality of the individual job that makes the most difference. A metal pan that isn't the right shape, or that has to be tweaked into position to fit the bike, isn't a whit better than a lightweight, flexible plastic bottom. You may also hear the complaint that fiberglass seat bases are prone to cracking, but this happens most often when the mounting hardware is allowed to work loose or when the fit of the seat to the bike is poor.

Cover Materials

Seat makers are deeply divided over the issue of leather or vinyl. A good-quality vinyl will have nearly the look and feel of leather. And yet this man-made product, sometimes called by the trade name Naugahyde, resists water intrusion, ultraviolet breakdown, and most kinds of rider-induced mayhem. It is, arguably, the better material for an all-weather seat. (Then again, if your bike gets garaged at the first hint of rain and never goes out in bad weather, long-term durability probably isn't your first consideration.) Vinyl comes in a variety of colors and textures.

Al Simmons, proprietor of Mustang Saddles, prefers to cover his H-D replacement saddles in the hide of the Nauga. It is almost impervious to weather and, according to Simmons, "will still look new in a couple of years, when leather seats have begun to discolor."

Says Bob Le Pera, "A lot of guys want leather to begin with, but when they see what we can do with vinyl, they're really surprised. We sell more than 70 percent of our seats in vinyl."

Then there's leather. "Like leather boots, the seat cover will conform to your body. After a while, it'll feel like the seat was made just for you," Corbin says. Corbin uses a variety of Connolly leathers, in smooth and basket-weave textures. You can also get leather in many patterns, and the odd snakeskin, eelskin, and, for all we know, schnauzerskin seat will show up on the custom trail.

And there seems to be little disagreement on this point: A well-broken-in leather saddle not only looks more substantial and impressive on the bike, but it feels cooler in warm weather and is more effective at wicking sweat away from the surface than vinyl.

While it's true that the overall shape and density of foam of any seat will be the main determiners of comfort, the cover plays a part. A thick, unyielding cover increases the apparent stiffness of the foam and may cause the seat to change its shape after a few hours on the road. Contrarily, a loose-fitting, thin cover often lacks necessary support for daylong comfort.

Seats for the Custom Inclined

As you can see, the variables in building a seat are many. So, as with any part of customizing your Harley, you should decide early on just what you want from your custom saddle. Are you primarily a short-hop rider, sticking to a dozen-mile

Below: **The Gunfighter for the Softail series is perhaps the best-selling of all Corbin saddles. A padded perch makes for a short-hop, two-up bike, but the main reason for the aft hump is styling continuity.**

Below: This custom seat by Stitcher uses minimal padding to preserve low seat height and the line of the bike. It is not likely to be a comfortable seat.

occasional commute and the Sunday-afternoon ride? If so, you can consider some of the new breed of saddles designed with looks as the primary factor. It's not to say that a stylish seat—particularly one that is thin and sleek, all the better to form itself to the bike—is going to be the equivalent of a bed of nails, but even the seat makers will admit that the thinner saddles are ill-suited to long rides.

A good example of this new breed of seat is Mike Corbin's Fast Gunfighter saddle. (It's available for all modern Harleys in a variety of colors and styles.) Taken from the traditional Gunfighter, this model has been trimmed of some of the foam from the forward part of the seating area. This offers the rider more room in front and helps reduce true seat height. Moreover, the Close version hugs the frame rails more affectionately—this required a new seat mold for Corbin—and has the pilot seating area pushed forward slightly, easing the reach to, say, a set of low drag bars. Corbin is the first to admit that the Close Gunfighter may not be as comfortable as the standard model, but it's what the market has demanded.

Taken a step further, Corbin's Hollywood Solo saddle is unabashedly about style first. Cut low and close to the frame, the Hollywood is thin and seems at first almost outrageously firm. Corbin says, quite bluntly, "This seat is about looking good, not 500-mile days."

Likewise, Le Pera's Silhouette seats are intended for the appearance-conscious crowd. Available for all current Big Twins and Sportsters (as well as the FXRs of old), the Silhouette aims to combine a broad base with minimal, firm padding to give a low seat height and that custom appearance. The Silhouette is available in two-up and solo versions.

Since riders continued to ask for even lower, sleeker seats, Le Pera introduced the Bare Bones seats. These models hug the frame rails ever more closely and have but a hint of padding; these are serious style-first saddles.

Danny Gray's Wedge seat and Mustang's Plain Cobra saddle are also among the style-is-best models, with a frame-hugging contour emphasis on low profile.

There are many more examples of custom-oriented seats in the dozens of catalogs out there. The sure tip-off that you're looking at an appearances-first saddle is when the description focuses on the look and close fit to the bike.

1. **This lean Mustang saddle fits FX-series Harleys and provides a low seat height in the bargain. It's made with a vinyl cover and uses firm, poured foam inside.**

2. **Pillow-look seats are still popular, particularly for the touring types. Here's Mustang's FL-series couch. Be sure to buy the right seat for your model-year bike. Harley has re-arranged under-saddle real estate more than once.**

3. **Gray's Wedge Cobra seat makes a point of following the fender line.**

4. **Not all seats have to be straightforward. This custom creation carries through a styling element of the bike.**

Above: **Corbin's Gambler saddle for the XL is made of leather and represents a sort of hybrid between the Hollywood Solo and a two-up Gunfighter. The small passenger pad is for short hops only.**

Right: **Many customizers seek out materials that match the overall color of the bike, which can give an uncommonly unified appearance.**

Seats for the Crossover Rider

What if you want a mix of attributes—good style with enough long-haul comfort to sustain an occasional short tour? Then you have to be a bit pickier. Stay away from those ultrathin saddles and look for models with more padding and, in particular, relatively firm foam. You may want to consider buying into a new trend in seats—silicone gel. These days, seat makers have more silicone laying around than the cast of *Baywatch,* but for better reasons.

This gel, which is normally sandwiched between layers of conventional foam, is impervious to the packing that afflicts all conventional foam seats to one degree or another. The advantage, of course, is that the foam and gel help distribute your weight across the surface of the saddle, rather than pinpointing it on protrusions on the seat base.

Then there's always another alternative: Buy more than one saddle. On most Harleys the seat swap is so easy that this tactic makes a lot of sense.

When you shop for a middle-ground seat, look for reasonably thick padding and a moderately large seating area. You may also want a pronounced backrest area—particularly you forward-foot-control types. Beware of extremely large backpads; some of these can force you into a single position on the bike, a sure recipe for premature butt burn.

Many aftermarketers manage to successfully combine good looks and decent comfort in one package. Mustang's Wide Regal Touring seat is considered a good compromise. You'll notice that it has considerably more padding than the so-called low-profile saddles and is more generously sized. Same for Drag Specialties' line of Double Bucket seats, Corbin's Gunfighter and Lady models, and Le Pera's Monterey Custom series.

Touring Types

Still other riders settle for nothing less than the ultimate in long-haul comfort—you FLT owners know who we're talking about. Here again, look for the saddle with reasonably firm padding, generous surface area, and modest cutouts or "pockets" in the form. This last item is a personal call, though, because some riders like to have the lower-back support provided by heavily bucketed seats. Others prefer not to be locked into one position for the duration of the trip.

Look for good internal support of the seat. Mustang's metal seat bases permit welded metal bolsters under the foam. This allows for a slightly softer padding without fear of the seat becoming grossly misshapen under a heavy rider.

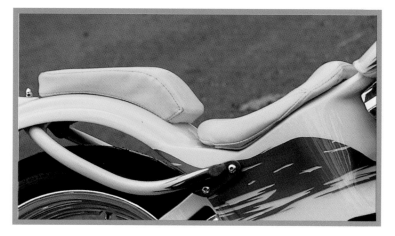

Fit and Finish

Once you've decided on a type of saddle—Saturday-night special or long-haul loafer—take some time to determine the overall quality of the seat. First, how does it feel as a piece of work? According to various seat authorities, you can learn a lot by just picking up the seat and feeling its heft. A light, wimpy seat probably won't last as long as something with a sturdy base and heavy innards.

Look at the stitching. Is it straight? Are the seams double- or triple-stitched? Most seat makers use what is called a French seam, in which one seam is sewn and then the material is folded over and the other seam goes on over the top, covering the first seam. This way you get the strength of two seams without the visual bulk. Whatever the type, pull on the seams and make sure they're tight and sturdy.

Peek underneath. Seat makers use a variety of methods to attach the seat cover to the base, from rivets to staples. It's generally agreed that rivets, preferably stainless steel, are sturdier. Feel around the edges to determine if any of the attaching hardware can be felt through the cover. Also notice how well the material has been trimmed. Although you can't see a ragged cut with the saddle installed, it can be an indication of the overall quality of the item.

Above: Le Pera's Silhouette vinyl saddle has been immensely popular; it's low and lean, yet surprisingly comfortable. Firm foam is the key.

Right: This Sportster's solo saddle includes a leather valance and decorative studs. Saddleman makes it.

Pay attention to the way the seat fits the bike. Despite appearances, there are actually several different seat patterns and mounting schemes in the Harley line. Attempting to fit a similar but different style of seat base to your bike is a bit like playing Scrabble with all the vowel tiles missing.

If you have to twist or otherwise mangle the seat to get it to line up with the stock mounting holes, you have either a bad seat or a bike made with slightly different mounting points (probably the former). While there are slight variations among Harleys in some dimensions, an aftermarket seat should fit with a minimum of fiddling.

Notice how the seat base mates with the bike. Here there is little agreement on the method, though, and you have to look at your particular installation to decide what's important. Mustang and Corbin, for example, use rubber bumpers to transfer part of the rider's weight to the frame. Corbin says this is the only way to go, since carpet or felt

can hold dirt against the paint, where vibration will soon turn the combination into scratches. Such a consideration makes the most sense where you will have the fender exposed; say, you use both solo and two-up saddles for your Road King. In any case, there should be ample padding to protect the painted surfaces.

1. This custom Saddleman saddle on a Springer Softail makes good use of the styling convention of following the rear fender and fender-rail lines with the base of the saddle.

2. A studded, two-up saddle from Harley provides enough real estate for the passenger, something not all replacement saddles offer. It's important to decide if passenger accommodations are a big deal for you. Many spouses refuse to ride on something the size of a soap bar—which may or may not be your intent.

On some custom seats, you'll be faced with the seat base being right on the painted rear fender. Make sure there's good-quality padding or carpet where the metal meets enamel, and be sure it's clean before you install the saddle.

Ultimately, choosing the right replacement saddle comes down to walking the lines between style and function and between budget and desire. There's much to choose from, and the chances are excellent that you'll find a seat with which you'll have a successful long-term affair. Just remember: It's an important decision. Make it wisely.

Above: **Heritage Softails done up in a more retro look often use larger saddles with studded valances.**

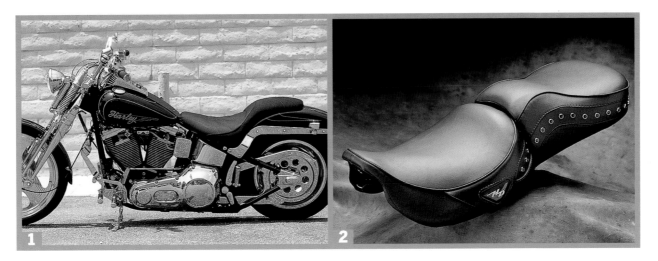

Chapter 4:

Handlebars & Foot Controls

While you might choose handlebars to present a certain look, consider how they will affect your use of the bike.

It's common to select handlebars and footpeg positions based on appearance—nothing wrong with that. But as you're perusing the catalogs and sneaking sideways glances at other Harleys, keep a few basic considerations in mind. The overall comfort and utility of your bike depends on the match between its seating position and your physique. For example, long, tall riders prefer a forward foot control because it gives them much-needed legroom. And for long-haul riders,

Opposite: Harley Springer models use different bar mounts from the rest of the line. These risers have been painted black. The upper clamps of the risers accommodate the normal 1-inch, Harley-style handlebar. Drag Specialties' speedometer complements the standard tank-mounted speedometer.

adding highway pegs or replacing floorboards with standard pegs can greatly increase endurance.

And while you might choose handlebars to present a certain look, consider how they will affect your use of the bike. If you ride every day, you probably don't really want super-tall apehangers because at highway speeds you'll feel more like a human sail than a cool cat. Also carefully consider the effects of a very low bar coupled with forward foot controls: Typically, this stretches out the lower back and places nearly all your weight on the saddle. If you don't have a good seat, you'll be unhappy with this arrangement. Most riders find that a moderately low, flat bar is the best all-around compromise between looks and function. (Of course, if you plan few trips of any distance, any seating position that fits you will work.)

Above: Forward foot controls and tall apehangers create a distinctive riding position reminiscent of the choppers of the 1960s and 1970s.

Left: Harley makes a series of dress-up kits for stock floorboards. These chrome-and-rubber inserts are far fancier than the plain black originals.

Key Handlebar Dimensions

All Harley handlebars are the same diameter—1 inch. You will also find bars with larger-diameter sections that run between the clamps and the handlebar controls for a beefy look.

Some other buying considerations:

Dimples. It's important that you buy handlebars with dimples for wiring if you have a 1982-or-later bike and intend to keep the stock Harley hand controls. The collars on the controls have no cutouts for the wiring, so the bar must make the accommodation. Bars for bikes from this era also are usually drilled for press-in wire holders.

Knurling. Stock Harley bars and many aftermarket bars have knurled sections that coincide with the clamp locations to provide a more secure footing. If you are opting for a relatively short bar—something in the drag style or low-rise variety—this knurling isn't

critical. But for taller bars, particularly apehangers, you really need the extra purchase provided by the knurling.

Finish. Harley uses polished stainless bars as its standard, but by far the top choice in aftermarket bars is chrome. You may also see black-chromed and painted-black bars hanging from the accessory-shop wall. As with any chrome accessory, check the finish carefully for scratches, blemishes, and evidence of lifting chrome.

Air-assist fittings. Harley's touring rigs and a few of the FXR-series bikes use air-assisted forks that also employ a pneumatic anti-dive circuit. It works by using the handlebar as an air reservoir; it's open to the fork system during normal riding. When the brakes are applied, a valve closes the connection to the bar, reducing the total air volume of the system and increasing the

1. **White Brothers' Beach bar is a wide, low device intended to recall the beach cruiser bicycles of the Beach Boys days.**

2. **Arlen Ness's late-style drag bars utilize fixed risers and deeply chromed tubing. The integral risers remove the opportunity to change the bar angle, though. As with all Ness designs, it's clean.**

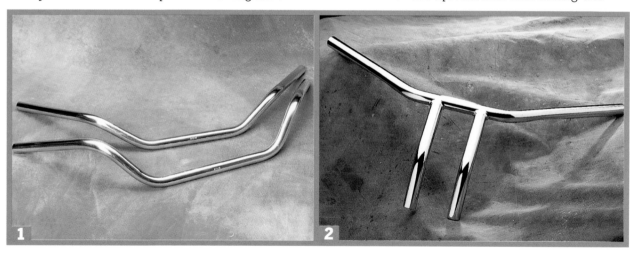

effective front-end spring rate. Should you elect to keep it—and many riders say the system's effects are subtle—you need handlebars with the appropriate fittings. You can also have the fittings added to the handlebar, but it's not an easy task.

Dimensions. Handlebars are described by several key dimensions. They are *overall width, rise, pullback,* and *center width.* Most of these are self-explanatory, but you should not ignore the information contained in the catalogs. Making more than a slight change in dimensions to the original bar requires quite a bit of work.

Making the Change

By far the most important concern in swapping bars is to make sure everything will fit. As a rule, you can replace your short bars with ones about 2 inches wider *or* with 2 inches more pullback *or* with 2 inches more rise. But not all of the above. The reason is that Harley does not provide much slack in the cables, front-brake hydraulic hose, or electrical connections to make an extensive change feasible without a lot of extra work.

The reverse situation—going from tall/wide bars to something smaller and narrower—is also worthy of forethought. While you can usually find a place to bundle the electrical wiring as long as you aren't

A wide, flat drag bar needs to have tall risers connecting it to the upper triple clamp to prevent interference with the fuel tank at maximum lock.

Right: Harley's standard 883 handlebar is not quite a drag bar because the shallow bends allow for the grips to clear the tank at full steering lock. A true drag bar on virtually any Harley requires taller risers.

Above: Bikes with central speedometers often receive a secondary tach on the handlebar clamp. Here, an H-D-built mechanical speedo is joined by an H-D electronic tach in a 50's Boy billet handlebar mount. This custom Softail also has a billet dashboard cover from Arlen Ness and stock hand controls and switch housings that have been chromed.

making extreme changes, you aren't likely to get the clutch and brake connections to fit properly. The solution is to buy a replacement clutch cable and front-brake line. While you are buying new hydraulic line, you really should take the opportunity to upgrade to braided steel lines. (See the Wheels & Brakes chapter for more information.)

There's no clever formula to use in deciding which length to specify when you order a new clutch cable and front brake line. Instead, you just have to buy the new bar, mount it to the bike, and install the hand controls without the brake line or clutch cable in place. Measure how much too short (or too long) the stock line and cables are and adjust accordingly. Be sure to measure at both left and right steering locks. In extreme cases, you might have to replace the throttle cables, too.

You can also get close by matching OEM parts. Let's say you have a Dyna Super Glide with the factory buckhorn but want the taller apehanger standard on the Dyna Wide Glide. If you use the stock FXDWG bar or a close approximation, you're safe going ahead and buying the clutch cable and aftermarket brake-line kit for the Wide Glide. Be careful when choosing the front-brake lines to remember if the equivalent bike has longer- or shorter-travel suspension than yours. It can make up to a 2-inch difference in total hose length.

This should be obvious, but in case it's not: Don't even consider stretching the original components beyond the 2-inch recommendation. A clutch cable that is stretched tight or a brake line that is improperly routed is an engraved invitation to disaster.

Use caution when selecting a handlebar bend. Here, a normal hand gets pinched between the grip and the fuel tank. Changing the bend of the bar or the bar's rotation in the clamp would fix this problem.

Is There Room?

Beyond deciding if the bars will work with the stock switch gear and connections, you need to ensure that the replacements won't contact any bodywork. Carefully measure the stock bars and compare those figures with the ones listed in the catalogs. Make sure that your calculations leave at least an inch from the controls to the fuel tank, as well as between the handlebar and any fairing pieces. There's no more disheartening sound than that of the switch housing making a dime-size dent in the tank.

So, What's Out There?

Check the catalogs and you'll see a stupefying range of handlebars. Conventional handlebars are available from Harley's P&A division, usually versions of the same bars used on the production line. Here you have the choice of the standard stainless finish, black paint, or chrome.

Chrome Specialties, Custom Chrome, Drag Specialties, and Nempco all carry a full line of handlebars, their own brands as well as the

Right: Springer risers can be had in the conventional configuration—with the bar directly atop the centerline of the riser—or with set-backs. These setbacks allow use of a straighter, drag-style bar. A small Drag Specialties tach is clamped to the handlebar; other mounting methods are available, including billet brackets that fit between the risers.

Above: Tidy wiring is vitally important, particularly if you use braided-steel wraps. Use clips wherever they're needed and keep the bare braid away from anything that moves.

highly regarded K&N line. Even the high-end customizers like Arlen Ness and Carlini's produce grippable artwork.

This is one of the few areas in accessorizing your Harley that you can let aesthetics take the tiller. For the purposes of pure function—that is, being able to do the job—a handlebar is pretty much a handlebar.

An increasingly popular choice is a bar with integral risers, also called a T-bar. Arlen Ness has a line of gorgeous bars, as do Custom Chrome, Drag Specialties, and White Brothers. And while these bars are undeniably good-looking, they carry a couple of inherent shortcomings that are worth mentioning. First, you have no way of adjusting their position; bolting as they do to the top triple clamp, there's no method of altering the angle of the bar relative to the fork. Second, if you have bar-mounted instruments, you'll need to find them another home. Naturally, Arlen and the others will sell you special riser instrument mounts for this

great adventure. Obviously, this isn't a problem for those of you with tank-mounted instruments, but keep it in mind in case you have plans for an add-on tachometer down the road.

Rise Above It All

An alternative to shelling out for the one-piece drag bars is to replace the stock riser with something snazzier. All Harley models use small pedestals that mount to the upper triple clamp through a set of bushings and a single bolt on each side. It's painless to replace the stock risers with something more elaborate. Harley P&A sells a set, in straight-up or curved styles, as do all of the major aftermarketers. There's really no science in getting a good riser—save for the usual caveat of remembering that you get what you pay for—as long as you add its height and pullback to the equation when determining if you can still use your stock clutch cable and front-brake line.

1. Drag Specialties makes smaller-than-stock instruments for custom applications. Here, the gauges are mated to a billet upper clamp/instrument mount, also from Drag.

2. Billet instrument housing holds a stock Harley speedometer on the left and a multigauge cluster from 50's Boy that indicates engine speed, oil temperature, oil pressure, and voltage.

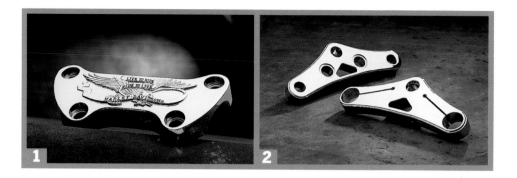

1. Harley's "Live to Ride" handlebar clamp. It replaces the standard, unadorned dog-bone piece.

2. Ness also makes a line of CNC-machined billet aluminum triple clamps. These replace Harley's standard cast clamps and offer hidden hardware. They are available in narrow-glide and wide-glide versions.

3. Mirrors are surprisingly hot items for bolt-on customizers. This one is one of Arlen Ness's most popular catalog items. Be certain the quality of the chrome finish is good and resist the temptation to buy silver dollar–size units. Also, note that most replacement mirrors use flat glass instead of the slightly convex glass that Harley employs normally; this narrows your field of view to the rear.

4. The grooves of this knurled-style grip provide a firmer grasp in wet weather. This is a Drag Specialties grip and a Jay Brake master cylinder.

As always, be looking for good-quality chrome, grade-eight bolts, and a complete hardware package. Also, if you are replacing the risers on a high-mileage bike, consider going with new rubber bushings; these things wear out after a while. Finally, resist the temptation to hard-bolt the handlebar riser to the upper triple clamp, particularly on bikes without rubber-mount engines. Those rubber doughnuts are there for a reason: to make the handlebar shakes tolerable. Eliminating that line of isolation could make your bike genuinely unpleasant to ride.

Levers and Things

Another highly popular bar-side addition is the billet instrument mount. It replaces in gleaming milled aluminum the workaday steel truss Harley normally fits; just be sure to ask if your instrument lights will fit properly. Harley has changed the bulb layout a couple of times over the years, so be sure to check.

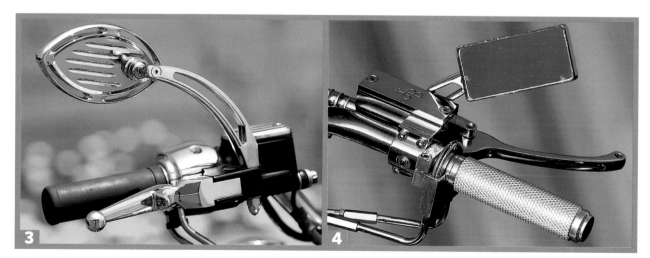

Also, you will be confronted with a bevy of replacement levers. Bear this in mind: Harley's rejection rate for chromed levers is extremely high, and for good reason. It's hard to control the application of chrome in an assembly-line environment. The total thickness of the lever is crucial to how well it fits the perch. As a side effect, many of the aftermarket levers tend to be loose in the perch—to allow for some increase in the part's thickness, even if the production department isn't sure precisely how much that will be.

When you buy an aftermarket lever, check the fit carefully and reject any that don't snuggle tightly into the perch.

Gripping Developments

It's amazing to consider the sheer mass of replacement handgrips, again from both Harley and the vast aftermarket. Because Harley hasn't changed the way the grips fit since the 1973 model year—and with precious few exceptions, one grip fits all models—there's an accessorizer's delight waiting in the catalogs.

1. Harley changed to these slightly revised hand controls in 1996. While the clutch lever is the same as before, the brake lever is new to accommodate a different brake-light switch. New, aerodynamically shaped switches became more water resistant than before. Harley immediately began offering chrome versions of these switches, but the aftermarket has caught up.

2. Aftermarket pre-1995 controls and switch housings can be had in black or chrome, like these. Many customizers prefer to chrome the stock Harley housings rather than buy non-Harley replacements. The quality of the switches in the aftermarket items has been uneven in the past. Inspect any you are considering with great care.

3. One way to disguise the handlebar hardware is to cover it. This Road King has a chromed-steel bar-clamp cover from 50's Boy.

"The choice of handgrip is not exactly a make-or-break item. If you don't like your purchase, no big deal; buy another set."

As with handlebar bends and paint schemes, the choice of handgrip is highly personal. (And because of the low price involved, it's not exactly a make-or-break item. If you don't like your purchase, no big deal; buy another set.) Keep a few basics in mind when shopping, though.

Solid billet handgrips *look* fantastic but—let's face facts here—they're less than the most functional way to mate gloved hand with motorcycle. Add even the slightest bit of water, and many of these billet grips turn slippery. If you forge ahead with the billet parts, remember to use a drop of blue LocTite on the set screws; these things are notorious for slipping off a hammering sled at inopportune moments.

Similarly, the open-cell foam grips tend to catch and hold water, which, if you live in colder climes, might mean ice on that early-morning ride. In between, there's tremendous variety, so you shouldn't have trouble fitting a grip to your overall styling plan. As mentioned before, if you are mainly a fair-weather, short-hop rider, a good compromise between the looks of the solid-metal grip and the utility of the solid-rubber version could be any of the hybrids. These are metal grips with segments of rubber inlaid to help improve grip.

Many riders find handgrips with a slightly barrel-shaped center more comfortable than the constant-diameter models. Harley sells a set under the Nostalgia label, and there are several more from the rest of the aftermarket. Finally, you might also see a slew of grips with leather surfaces. These really look great when they're new, but you should be aware that it takes a commitment to keep them preserved and out of the sun whenever possible to keep them from fading. Eventually, they *will* fade, but you can postpone the onset with care.

Foot Controls

Several Harley models have arrived from Milwaukee with forward foot controls. This theme derives from the highway pegs mounted on the front downtubes to provide a bit of variety for the old dogs. Forward foot control conversions are extremely popular, and several manufacturers are in the field. Arlen Ness makes a couple of sets, as do

1. **Arlen Ness billet "twister" grips are for the hard-core stylist. Solid grips look great but transmit more vibration to the rider and are often too slippery in the wet.**

2. **Harley's cushion grips provide a thick, soft grip. Riders with small hands may prefer the thinner-diameter standard grips.**

3. **Drag Specialties' chrome levers are available for the late-style, 1996-and-later hand controls.**

Custom Chrome, JayBrake, Legends, Performance Machine, UMI, and others. Because these controls are relatively easy to build from billet, many independent shops have begun to make their own, too.

They are easy to install, also, because of Harley's almost religious devotion to parts commonality. All Dyna Glide and FXR chassis come with the bosses for highway pegs already on the frame, which makes retrofitting forward controls relatively easy.

As is always true, judge a set of controls on its looks. Clean chrome, well-finished machining, and first-rate fasteners are all items to watch for. Also, pay particular attention to the bearings or

1. The shifter side of the PM forward controls shows the pivot point aft and above the footpeg. Try to find controls in which the shifter pivot is near your ankle pivot, as seen here. This keeps the shift pedal from dragging across your boot. The brake side uses the same pedal but also provides a mount for a PM brake cylinder.

2. Storz makes this rearset shifter kit for the XL. A double joint allows this setup to keep the conventional shift pattern. Previous examples used a simple lever on the normal shift shaft, resulting in a racing-style pattern with first gear up and the rest down.

3. Twin O-ring footpegs provide some options for your feet. Be cautious placing two sets of pegs together so that there's no interference with the shift lever or brake pedal.

Softail passenger pegs are positioned by the frame hardpoints, but a lot of passengers prefer a different location. These Custom Chrome relocating plates accomplish the task.

bushings used. The control pivots should have generous bearings and nylon where the caps touch the bearing housings. More importantly, these bushings or bearings should be snug—you don't want any discernible axial movement—without binding.

Look for a shift-lever pivot near where your ankle would be. That's the natural pivot point of your foot. If the shift lever pivots in another location, it will rake the lever pad across your foot when you shift. It doesn't feel particularly good, nor will this tendency lead to long boot life. Stock Harley forward controls, though ordinary, got this detail right. Look for other sets that do, too.

Also, if you're starting with a bike that came stock with midfoot—that is, not foot-forward—controls, make sure you get a replacement set of primary cover panels. You will have to plug the hole the midcontrol shifter used in both the outer and inner primary cases. Budget the money and time for this detail.

Finally, remember that more times than not, you get what you pay for. Pieces of the bike that integrate with the shifting and braking are not the best items to skimp on.

Replacement Footpegs and Floorboards

As with handgrips, the aftermarket is about overflowing with replacement footpegs and floorboards, all in the name of sprucing up your bike's appearance. The same warning applies to solid billet footpegs as for similar handgrips. These are fair-weather items only, best left to the bike that never intentionally sees a drop of rain. Alternatives to this billet look include the many hybrid models, which manage to combine the glamour of a billet piece with the practicality of a rubber-shod item. When you're shopping this aisle, be sure you're willing to pay for the quality items. Cheap footpegs that have poorly designed rubber inserts are almost as bad as the raw item. Look for deep grooves for the inserts as well as the presence of thick, tough rubber.

4. Harley's O-ring shifter pedal kit matches the company's O-ring pegs.

5. UMI Racing builds a wide range of forward foot controls. When buying any controls, look for generous bearing areas and slop-free fittings like these. Any movement in the bearings will be felt by your foot and amplified by the long lever arm of the shift and brake pedals.

1. Rearset footpegs aren't common on Harleys, but Storz Performance's billet set has been popular among riders wanting a racier appearance for their Sportsters. An articulating linkage and relocated master cylinder make the rear brake installation feasible.

2. Built to match the twister handgrips are these like-named footpegs. Undeniably sexy in their chromed billet splendor, the pegs may nevertheless not be the ideal item for all-weather and touring riders.

3. A popular replacement for the utilitarian stock pegs are these O-ring pegs from Harley P&A. They're better than solid metal pegs in the wet but not quite as comfortable as the stock (if squishy) Harley items.

Right: Harley's floorboard insert kit can be installed quite easily, thanks to the generous use of original hardware and mounting points.

Far right: It's not just the rider who gets the cool floorboards. Insert kits are available for the passenger boards as well.

Opposite: Arlen Ness makes an astonishingly popular floorboard kit. This chromed-billet item uses rubber inserts to provide a modicum of traction, but you need to be careful of scratching the boards with dirty boot soles. These boards are much longer than the stock items.

Understand that the swap to sleeker footpegs will usually mean more vibration transmitted to your feet. If you're in the minority of riders who wear thick-soled boots, that's probably not going to be much of a problem. But thin-sole shoes or boots will faithfully transmit this newfound vibration right to your foot; and it won't feel nearly as good as some Las Vegas–style 25-cent vibrating bed.

Kury Akyn's Iso-Pegs were among the first footpegs to bridge the gap between appearance and function—there are, predictably, several knockoff products around now. Thick rubber cleats are sandwiched between chrome spacers for a custom look. They are also nearly as effective at damp-ing vibration as the stock items and are far less "squishy," a strong endorsement for riders who dislike the vague-feeling OEM bits.

There is a reason the stock Harley footpegs are squishy soft. They are designed to limit the vibra-tion transferred to your feet. They may not feel great or look stunning, but they work.

Same deal with floorboards. The main advan-tage of replacing footpegs with floorboards is that you get a lot more flexibility as to where you can put your feet. There's a good reason all Harley's touring models come standard with floorboards. As original equipment goes, Harley's floorboards are pretty good. They're just not very sexy, what

with their plain, stamped-steel frames and nondescript rubber pads.

Naturally, the aftermarket has plenty of alternatives. Again, be sure to get something with at least a little bit of rubber on the topside. Moreover, think through the kinds of trips you're likely to take. The lovely billet floorboards, like the immensely popular Ness-Tech items that are de rigueur on show bikes, tend to scratch easily if you aren't careful about getting all the rocks out of the soles of your boots. For long-distance riders, full rubber tops are a better bet.

There is one downside to floorboards, and that has to do with cornering clearance. If you've already lowered your bike and then decide to add floorboards, use caution on the first few rides. The wider boards, which also tend sit closer to the asphalt due to their mounting schemes, can really eat up the lean angle.

A Word on Mounts

Buying the correct footpeg is straightforward. Harley uses only three basic configurations, one male size and two females. (Both females use the same mount, $5/8$ inch between the flanges. The larger peg has a larger diameter.) The male mount is the one most likely to be on your bike in the rider's position; the male mount also is used for passenger pegs and as the rider's pegs on some forward-control bikes, though others employ the larger female size.

You will also see the pegs listed as large and small. Again, the large is intended to replace the main rider's pegs on midmount bikes, while the smaller version is closer to the dimensions of the passenger pegs and rider's peg on forward-mount controls. You can, of course, mix and match the sizes as you please.

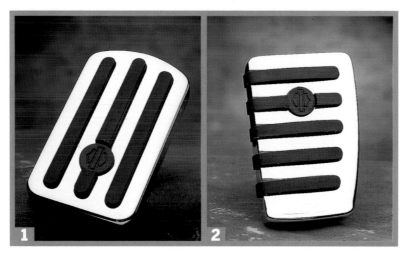

1. **Harley's brake-pedal dress-up kit replaces the standard plain rubber piece with the same mounting hardware.**

2. **Harley's brake-pedal cover kit comes in either horizontal or vertical orientation.**

Installing Handlebars

Replacing your handlebar is an easy Sunday-afternoon job, provided you have done your homework. First, you will have decided that your new handlebar is fairly close in size to the one you're tossing—that way you won't need to replace the clutch cable and brake hose, nor will you need to extend the stock handlebar wiring harness.

(If you do really want a much taller bar, it's no big deal. Just buy a wiring-harness extender and remember that it's better to solder the connections than to rely solely on the crimped connectors. Plan to replace both the clutch cable and the front-brake hose. You may also need to get creative in rerouting the throttle cables, though a very large change in bar length or width will call for new cables.)

The trick to making a bar change painless is to remove everything from the bar in advance. It's tough to balance a loose bar with all of the paraphernalia hanging from it. Start by removing the switch housings. Depending on the model-year of your bike, you may need a small Allen or Torx wrench. Loosen the switch halves and separate them from the bar. Then remove the clutch-lever perch by loosening the two screws that face rearward.

On the throttle side, you'll need to remove the cables. For bikes built in 1996 and later, the throttle ferrules are a press fit into the lower housing. Earlier bikes have threaded cable-sleeve ends. Remove the ends of the cables and their little brass ends from the nylon throttle sleeve. Be careful with these items, because they tend to jump from your now-greasy fingers. Remove the brass ends and pull the cables free.

If you're planning to change the front brake line, go ahead and loosen the fitting with a 12-point socket or box-end wrench. It's better to have suctioned the remaining fluid out of the reservoir first. Even so, have plenty of rags on hand to catch any brake fluid that may spill from the fitting. *Remember that this fluid corrodes paint.* If you don't intend to change the brake line, loosen the nearby mounting screws and clamps so you can move it away from the bar without bending the rigid line. Remove the right-side perch and switch housing.

Now that the bar's naked, you can simply loosen the four Allen bolts on the clamp and remove the bar. The right handgrip will come off with the throttle sleeve. You can get the other one off by gently prying with a long screwdriver or, better yet, by supplying compressed air to the opposite end of the bar. (If your bar has drilled holes to accommodate wiring clips, you'll need to tape them over or hold a finger atop the holes.) Apply just enough air pressure to walk the grip off the bar. Make sure the bar is not pointed at your faithful pet or a loved one.

Remember when you place the new bar in the clamps to align the serrated sections with the jaws of the clamp. Also, make sure you tighten the forward clamp bolts first so that the flat portions of the upper and lower clamps meet. Then torque the rearmost bolts to around 20 foot-pounds.

Reverse the removal procedure to reinstall the switch and lever components, being careful to not trap any wires under clamps. Use a diluted mixture of soap and water to lubricate the left handlebar end while you slide the grip in place.

Four coarse-thread bolts hold the handlebar in place. Note the location of the gap between the two clamp halves; usually it's at the rear. Reinstall the bars with the same clamp orientation.

Chapter 5:

Powertrain

Many other motorcycle makers have tried to emulate the Harley style and charisma, but none has been able to copy the raw-edged, low-rpm thunder of the Milwaukee twins.

Harley-Davidson motorcycles are unique in the world of consumer goods in many ways, but perhaps never more so than in the engine department. The gleaming V-twin engine, with 45 degrees between the cylinders, is an industrial icon. Many other motorcycle makers have tried to emulate the Harley style and charisma, right down to using narrow-angle powerplants, but none has been able to copy the raw-edged, low-rpm thunder of the Milwaukee twins.

Having the cylinders splayed 45 degrees from each other, together with the inline arrangement of the crank pins, gives both a distinctive sound and type of vibration. (Most of the Japanese V-twins utilize connecting rods that ride side-by-side on a large crank journal; this introduces another vibration mode called rocking couple.)

For most riders, it's Harley's adherence to its unique engineering tradition that is the prime at-traction. Harley engines by design provide bucketsful of low-end power, thanks in part to the long-stroke configuration of the engine, which in

Left: Harley switched over to the constant-velocity Keihin 40mm carburetor because it worked better with the lean mixtures required to meet emissions regulations. Big Twins got the carb in 1990, Sportsters in 1988. There are many ways to tune this carburetor to work adequately with mildly modified Big Twins and Sportsters, but a lot of riders dislike the slightly lazy throttle response.

Opposite: Evolution came to the Sportster line in 1986. By 1992, Harley took the opportunity to completely rework the bottom end as it fitted a five-speed transmission in place of the four-cogger. Although the Evo Sportster and Big Twins share a familiar face, few parts actually interchange.

Above: The classic Evolution Big Twin engine. Introduced in 1984, it is the powerplant that saved Harley. Reliable, capable of decent power gains, and an excellent cruising partner in a mild state of tune, the Evo has been a standout engine. One of the first iterations of the Evo was in the FXR chassis, now supplanted by the rubber-mount Dyna Glide.

turn calls for small valves and small, fast-burning combustion chambers. Properly tuned, a Harley engine is a model of flexibility, pulling cleanly from just above idle and providing enough torque that you can pretty much clank it into one gear and leave it there.

Because Harley has been making the Evolution engine since 1984 in Big Twin guise and 1986 in Sportster form, it has become by far the most common on the road. Today, most tuners are more familiar with the Evo than the previous engine families, even though they share many parts and are separated by just a branch or two on the tree of technology. It is because the Evo has been so popular that the lion's share of aftermarket parts are tailored for it, with a gradually decreasing supply and selection for the older mills.

The variety of aftermarket parts designed to give you more power from your Evolution engine is nothing short of breathtaking. That's why this section will concentrate on the basics of peeling the first layer of horsepower restrictions from your Big Twin or Sportster engine. There are many other books aimed at modifying or building Harley engines for racing or high-performance street applications; your local dealer or speed emporium can suggest the right tome for you. What follows will give you a basic understanding of how to extract more (and usable) power from your Harley that should not, if the work is performed correctly, adversely affect reliability or longevity.

Flow Basics

All internal-combustion powerplants can be thought of as air pumps. The more air you can move through the system—which includes the intake and exhaust tracts as well as the cylinder head and valves—the more power that engine will produce. Anything that restricts or does not optimize airflow—the carburetor, airbox, mufflers, or camshaft design—will curtail power output.

But if it were easy to cram lots of air into the engine and extract the maximum quantity on the other end, every shadetree tinkerer would be a master tuner. Here's the rub: In addition to good mass flow of air, that air must maintain good velocity throughout the rev range to retain decent drivability characteristics. An engine with gaping ports, huge carburetors, and a wide-open exhaust probably will not have good air velocity at low rpm—though the setup is certainly capable of big flow numbers at high rpm. That makes for a recalcitrant beast around town.

Obviously, then, it's not such a lead-pipe cinch to get big horsepower numbers out of the average Harley Big Twin mill. What separates the true maestros of tuning from the catalog-page-flipping hacks is an understanding of one thing: balance. Every component has to work in concert, and every piece in the engine's airflow path must complement another. A yawning, wide-open exhaust will not work well with a stuffed-up carburetor and airbox, and a stock, extremely mild camshaft.

Keep this concept of balance in mind when you select hop-up components for your bike. Doing so

Above: S&S is a household name in Harley speed parts. Here, the company's famous teardrop air cleaner plays center stage to the Softail's engine. S&S also sells complete engine packages. Good performance tuning will retain the engine's inherent low-end power bias and merely increase the output without making the engine unreliable or difficult to control.

Left: The Evolution Big Twin as installed in the Dyna Glide chassis. There's little evidence from the outside that this could be a large-displacement modification of the normally 80-cubic-inch engine. Two finishes are available—the as-cast, silver version like this, and one coated in wrinkle-finish black paint.

A modern Evolution Big Twin in mildly modified form, featuring an Edelbrock Qwiksilver carburetor (hiding under the replacement air filter), Bartels exhaust system, and hotter camshaft. With a rumble and swagger that have yet to be copied, the Evo pounds out low-rpm torque like few other engines. This one, with modest modifications, is a charismatic yet tractable performer.

1. Unit-construction engines (that is, non–Big Twins) in Harleys have been winning on racetracks for more than four decades. Repli-racers like this Storz bike take the standard Evo Sportster engine and put it in place of a more cantankerous racing powerplant—a fine idea for the street. Notice that the Storz exhaust routes the head pipes sinuously around the engine to achieve equal-length pipes.

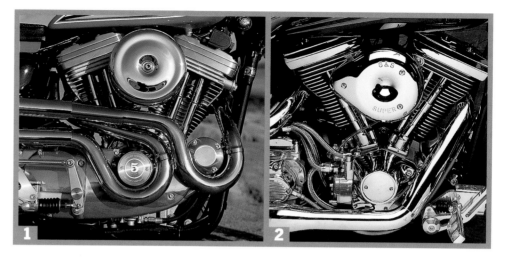

will greatly increase your chances of success and happiness with the mods.

Before modifying your Harley engine, think about your ultimate goal. Do you want a dragstrip demon, a fire-breathing machine capable of showing its taillight to anything on two or four wheels? (Maybe you *think* you do, but talk to someone who's built such a beast; chances are he'll recommend something milder.) Know the tradeoffs. A seriously hot, large-inch Evo engine will be nowhere near as reliable or tractable as a more mild mill. Many new riders who think they want all the power that can be had from the Harley engine end up seriously disappointed.

A far more rational approach is to apply conservative tuning techniques that offer nearly half again as much horsepower as a stock engine, but with no noteworthy reduction in durability. On the cost/benefit bell curve, you want to be at the point where the engine is making the most power before the reliability plot heads downhill. For general reference, this is in the neighborhood of 75 to 80 horsepower for a stock-displacement Big Twin. More important, though, is that your engine have a broad, useful torque curve. Horsepower looks great on a piece of paper, but torque is what makes the bike *feel* fast and powerful.

Mild Out of the Box

More hop-up parts are available for both Evolution engine families than anything this side of a small-block Chevy V-8. It's worth answering the question of *why* such an extensive Harley speed-enhancing aftermarket is necessary in the first place. The answer is that Harley has been able to bring the venerable V-twin into conformity with today's federal emissions and noise regulations only with herculean effort. Harley engineers readily admit that every year the most difficult assignment from management is to keep the air-cooled motors on the right side of the law.

While emissions requirements can often be met with lean fuel mixtures, retarded ignition timing, tame camshaft profiles, and catalytic converters, the noise issue is the most difficult nut for Harley to crack. Air cooling calls for generous cylinder clearances—the expansion rates of the cylinder and piston are vastly different, so accommodation must be made for sufficient cold clearances to prevent scuffing while still maintaining useful running (hot) clearances. These broad clearances lead to noise. Current methods of testing for noise-emissions compliance impose a disadvantage on Harley. With the intake and exhaust systems and cam drive all on the same side of the bike, all the big noise producers are close together and create a noise "footprint" heavily biased toward the right side of the bike. Because the noise testing sets a limit for any *one* microphone, Harley really gets put behind the engineering eight ball.

2. Softail engines are identical to the Dyna Glide, FL-series, and FXR mills, save for details of the primary case design and oil-tank location. Harley produces just one "power unit" for all Big Twin models. This bike has an S&S carburetor and air cleaner, as well as chrome lifter blocks and a plain billet timing cover. One of the beauties of the Harley Big Twin is that it's hard to tell if you have a stock-displacement 80-cubic-inch engine or something considerably larger—and meaner.

The Return of Screamin' Eagle

Until recently, Harley's Screamin' Eagle product line had taken a low profile in catalogs and promotions, although the parts have been available through dealers all along. At the introduction of the 1998 model Harley-Davidsons, the company's in-house Parts & Accessories spokesman, Tom Parsons, emphasized that Harley is not about to get left behind in the vast aftermarket for performance parts. Further, Harley has stated unequivocally that Screamin' Eagle components will be the first aftermarket parts available for any new Harley models.

FUEL-INJECTION MODS

To illustrate its point, Harley's P&A division introduced new components for the fuel-injected models that no one in the aftermarket had developed. These new performance packages take advantage of a change in programming Harley has made to all new fuel-injected models. New for 1997 was a system that allowed after-the-fact calibration changes. The first generation of Harley's EFI, used through 1996, was not capable of being altered to accommodate a freer-flowing engine.

Screamin' Eagle has two basic packages for the EFI models. The Stage I kit includes a freer-flowing air-filter element, a reprogrammed EFI cartridge, and a revised breather kit. For the 1997-and-later models, this mod runs about $250; for earlier bikes, which need a new fuel-injection computer, the kit is about $550. Harley promises a 10 percent improvement in torque—as well as a broader torque curve—and a 5 HP increase. (These numbers are taken at the crankshaft—rear-wheel figures will be 15 percent or so lower—and come from bikes with the stock exhaust system. Freer-flowing pipes or mufflers ought to add measurably to these improvements.)

A second level, called Stage II, adds a more aggressively ground camshaft and high-flow fuel injector nozzles. This kit runs $500 for the 1997-and-later bikes and $800 for the earlier models. Harley claims a 15 percent torque increase (to just over 90 foot-pounds at 4000 RPM) and a boost of just more than 10 HP compared with the stock bike. Again, these increases are based on using the stock exhaust system—

additional gains can be expected with freer-flowing pipes or mufflers. Both Screamin' Eagle kits are approved for on-road use in all fifty states. This is unlikely to be true for most of the aftermarket items.

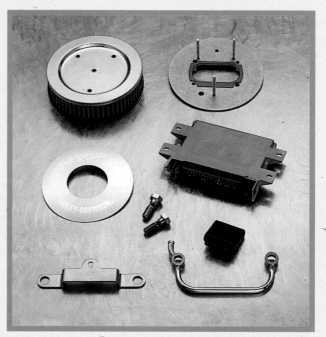

Above: **Harley's Screamin' Eagle EFI kits include replacement air-cleaner backing plates, filter element, breather assembly, and revised computer control chips. These systems allow the stock Harley fuel-injection system to pump out more fuel, and thereby more horsepower, than stock. The nature of the H-D injection setup means that adding freer-flowing exhausts and air filter and a hotter cam requires system recalibration.**

So to meet the federally mandated limits, Harley has, over the years, further strangled the induction and exhaust systems. It has also used tame cam profiles and tight cam-drive-gear tolerances to reduce mechanical noise.

The result is that a current Evolution Big Twin puts out about 50 to 55 HP and has restricted high-rpm thrust, but the low-end and midrange torque figures are quite good. Still, anyone who's done any engine work on an Evolution engine knows there's much more lurking in the long-stroke, two-valve engine.

The Three Major Elements of More Power

The performance of Evolution-engine Harley-Davidsons is held back by restrictive air filters and exhaust pipes as well as mild cams and an ignition-based rev-limiter that's designed to help prolong engine longevity by shutting off spark just beyond 5,000 rpm. High-velocity air makes a lot of noise; that's why Harley has had to cork up the engines to stifle what *we* would call music but the feds term noise.

Happily, the first stage in engine improvements is both one of the least expensive and one of the most effective. It comes down to three basic items: air cleaner replacement combined with rejetting the stock carb, and muffler and ignition module replacement. You should perform the first two steps simultaneously to reap the full benefits.

Secondary stages of improvements come from a new camshaft (or four new ones, if you ride a Sportster), an aftermarket carburetor, increased displacement, and, possibly, some cylinder-head modifications. (Alternatively, many riders are turning to new head assemblies in lieu of modifying the stock part.)

There are, of course, further levels of modification, including outrageously large engines, turbocharging, supercharging, and nitrous injection, as well as radical cams and compression ratios so high you'll need aviation gas to make the bike run. But these are engines for certifiable power junkies; they are, as mentioned earlier, temperamental, difficult-to-ride engines that should never really venture outside the racetrack.

Stage 1: Carb, Air Cleaner, Ignition, and Pipe

For your stock-displacement Big Twin or 1200cc Sportster, this first stage of modifications will deliver by far the greatest bang for the buck. It's the easiest to perform and the kindest to your wallet.

For 883 Sportster owners, the following modifications will indeed perform well, but this model's upgrade to the full 1200cc displacement is so easy and cost-effective that it should be one of your first alterations. The main difference between the 1200 and 883 Sportsters is ½ inch in bore; the bottom ends and

An Arlen Ness–sculpted engine is ready to go into a custom chassis. There's nothing to say you can't build a high-performance, big-inch engine like this one for your stock-chassis Harley.

transmissions are identical. The 883 has marginally shorter gearing to offset its power deficit, and slightly smaller valves and ports. Removing the stock 883 cylinders and having them bored by an accomplished shop is straightforward. Then add a set of special, dish-head pistons and you're done. (You can't use the stock 1200 pistons because the 883's smaller combustion chamber would yield an unworkably high compression ratio.).

More Air for the Carburetor

This step will improve airflow to the carburetor. Many companies offer replacement air filters and airboxes. Keep in mind that while the stock Harley air filter is not optimum for airflow, it's the air cleaner and associated hardware that are really the culprits—again, in the name of managing noise.

Many suppliers provide replacement airboxes and less-restrictive air-filter elements. In replacing the stock air cleaner, you must relocate the engine breather assembly, too. Harley has fiddled with this setup for many years, hoping to reach the best compromise between venting crankcase pressures—which vary wildly in a long-stroke vee engine—without venting excessive amounts of oil

1. **The stock Harley air cleaner and filter element are particularly restrictive, in part to help curb noise emissions. Believe it or not, a 1200cc or 1340cc engine is expected to breathe through a slot in the lower edge of the air-cleaner backing plate about the size of a ballpark frank. The paper filter is disposable, unlike the reusable oil-gauze K&N.**

2. **Every carburetor needs a free-flowing filter. The Mikuni kit comes with a circular K&N filter element and a metal backing plate that joins with the stock air-cleaner cover.**

3. **One of the beauties of Harley's engine architecture—particularly the large air cleaner on the right side of the engine—is the opportunity to do some stealth tuning. Hidden behind the chrome air-cleaner inserts is a Mikuni HSR 42; note the U-shaped breather apparatus that replaces the stock plastic air cleaner–backing plate.**

4. **Kury Akyn's Hypercharger air cleaner uses forward-facing scoops to feed cool air to the carburetor. Don't expect much ram-air effect, though. There are a number of colored or styled inserts available.**

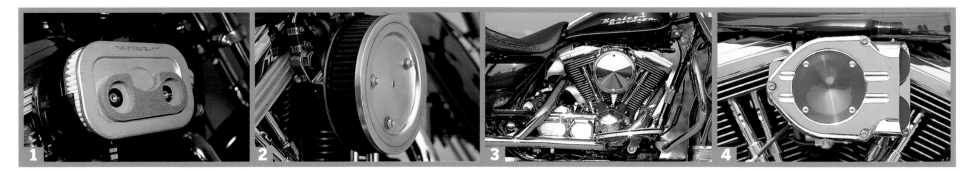

mist to the atmosphere. Before you buy a replacement air cleaner, make sure a breather assembly is available for your specific bike and model year. There are significant year-to-year differences, so you should pay attention to this detail. By 1993, Harley had settled on the through-head breather system, which is still in use on the 1998 models.

Simple, round air cleaners that house an oil-impregnated foam or K&N filter are among the most popular kits. You may also have seen Kury Akyn's scoop-like air box with forward-facing butterfly valves. Though you may hear some riders claim extra power from the "ram-air" effect of these portals, it's unlikely there's much extra thrust to be had. In perfect, undisturbed air, the pressure rise at 60 MPH is negligible. Even so, these airboxes work well for the same reason many other aftermarket units do—they flow more air than the stock air cleaner.

Perhaps the most popular element sold today is the K&N. This oiled-gauze filter maintains remarkable freedom from clogging even in the worst conditions. Moreover, K&N claims that the pleated element helps to align the airflow so the carburetor does not have to inhale turbulent air. A lot of mechanics are skeptical of this supposed trait. Most say that the K&N's overall high flow rate is what makes the filter line attractive.

Harley's own Screamin' Eagle brand of air cleaner conversions—which include new backing plates, filter elements, and the appropriate breather apparatus—are also available. They use the bike's original outer air-cleaner cover, but because the backing plate is much smaller—affording much greater potential airflow—these air cleaners are as effective as any of the aftermarket units using the K&N filter element.

Joker Machine makes a series of billet air cleaners in this triangular motif. They come with the appropriate breather kit and a washable foam element for Big Twins.

Right: Ball-milled styling is featured heavily here: The air-cleaner insert, points cover, floorboards, and brake-cylinder cover are all reproduced in this style by Ron Sims.

1. Custom Chrome's Siren covers are principally for altering the appearance of your bike, but when used with free-flow backing plates and filter elements, they can provide performance improvements as well.

2. Arlen Ness's billet air cleaner fits over the top of a standard S&S backing plate.

Now, More Fuel

Once you have opened up the intake side, you will need to deliver more fuel through the carburetor. There are several avenues to follow here. The first and most expedient is to recalibrate the stock Keihin 40mm constant-velocity carburetor with larger jets that flow more fuel. This is by far the least expensive method, although some fussy tuners dislike working with the standard mixer. It's true that many of the aftermarket carbs permit finer tuning than the standard carb, but unless you intend to increase the displacement of your bike beyond the stock 80 cubic inches, the stock carb will work fine.

You may also hear some carburetor manufacturers claim big power increases with their models. But according to an extensive body of dynamometer work performed by Jerry Branch's Branch Flowmetrics, there's precious little difference in power between a properly calibrated stock carb and the aftermarket carbs on a mildly tuned engine.

For most of his testing, Branch used the immensely popular Mikuni HSR 42 carb, a flat-slide design that's popular in racing circles.

Branch did so for the same reasons you might want to install the Mikuni (or one of the other aftermarket carbs) as one of the first mods: He knew his test engine was going to be pushed to ever-higher states of tune and wanted to have the one carb that would work through all the levels already in place. So if you know that you'll eventually take your Big Twin or Sportster into big-inch land, go ahead now with one of the aftermarket offerings. (However, if your tuning intentions re-

main modest, buying a high-end carb now is a waste of money.)

Get a jet kit—sometimes called a recalibration kit—for the standard Keihin constant-velocity carb. Harley has used this carb on the Big Twins since about 1989 and on the Sportster since 1987. These kits include replacement main jets—a brass metering orifice that determines the amount of fuel the carb will deliver at large throttle openings. The kits may also come with new pilot jets—these jets meter fuel at small throttle openings—different, adjustable needles, and a replacement return spring for the diaphragm-operated slide.

These parts can be installed in about an hour. Just make sure that you follow the directions explicitly and plan to stay at the baseline settings recommended by the recalibration-kit maker. Many of these kits include parts for hotter engines, so there will be jets that will be too large for what you need initially.

1. S&S's Super E is a straightforward butterfly carb with no slides or diaphragms. It's easy to tune but can be difficult to adjust to work perfectly in all engine ranges.

2. Installing an S&S carburetor on a bike that originally came with the Keihin CV carb requires a flange-style manifold in place of the normal spigot mount. This is S&S's own manifold for the Super E on a Big Twin.

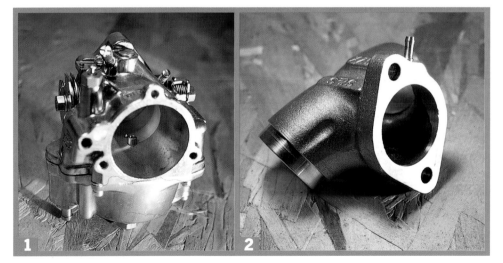

Below: SuperTrapp's ever-popular two-into-one system for Evolution Sportsters employs equal-length head pipes and a deep collector. (This system is also available for Big Twin models, in either the satin finish shown, stainless, or chrome.)

Choosing the Right Camshaft

Picking the wrong cam can have a far more negative effect on power than choosing the wrong pipe or carburetor. In an attempt to clear the air, a few basic questions were asked of the leading cam makers. You might be surprised at some of their answers.

First, you should understand some basic camshaft terminology. How a cam influences the performance of your bike is directly related to its physical properties. Not only is the size and shape of the cam lobe important, but so is the relationship of the lobe centers to one another and to the position of the piston. *Lift* describes how far the cam will move the lifter body. In modern Harleys, this distance is multiplied by 1.6 at the rocker arm to create the total valve lift. For stock-displacement Big Twins without any porting work, the experts recommend a cam with no more than .500 to .510 inches of lift. Any more is wasted because the heads simply cannot flow enough air to make use of the extra lift.

Duration signifies the period, expressed in crankshaft degrees, during which the valve is at least partly open. *Overlap*, also expressed in degrees of

1-2. Big Twin cams carry four lobes on a single shaft. A long-duration, long-overlap cam like this Andrews part makes for great high-rpm performance at the expense of low-end grunt. A too-loose cam drive will rattle, which is more of an annoyance than a mechanical problem, but a too-tight gear can break teeth. Pro shops know how to measure the cam-gear diameter to determine if you need a different gear for the replacement cam.

1

2

crank rotation, is the period during which both the exhaust and intake valves in a given cylinder are slightly open. As a general rule, the more lift, duration, and overlap a particular cam has, the more it will improve high-rpm power at the expense of low-end and midrange.

For reference: A typical stock Big Twin cam has about 200 degrees of duration and about 11 degrees of overlap—and a few of the California models have milder cams yet, upon which the lobes appear a mere afterthought. When coupled with the restrictive stock intake and exhaust systems, the mild cam is essential to making the best of a difficult situation. But that doesn't mean you have to live with it.

Ben Kudon of V-Thunder (the Harley-line subsidiary of Competition Cams) draws these approximate guidelines: "A cam with between 220 and 230 degrees of duration will benefit the low-end; from 240 to 250 degrees will mainly bump up the midrange; and a cam with more than 260 degrees of duration will boost top-end primarily. A cam with less than 30 degrees of overlap will also be good for low-end." Most popular "bolt-in" cams—cams that don't require special valve springs, extensive machining of the engine cases, or high-performance lifters—use between .470 and .500 inches of lift.

According to the cam makers, riders frequently make grievous mistakes in cam selection, almost always in the direction of buying too "hot" a cam. "You'd be surprised how many guys will try to put a drag-race cam in a street bike," says John Andrews, of Andrews Products. "It's the worst thing you can do." Instead of reaching for dyno-shredding top-end power, "Riders should be looking for the cam that will give you the best all-around powerband," says Rick Ulrich, of Crane Cams.

Within the milder-is-better landscape, riders also should keep in mind the weight of their bike—is it a comparative lightweight like a base Dyna, or a fully laden bagger? "In addition to compensating for the weight of the bike," says Ulrich, "think about how often you ride two-up and how often solo." You can choose a different powerband for a light bike, which will not seem dodgy with a sporting cam, whereas a bagger would. Heavy bikes should have cams that work at the lower end of the powerband. "Forget about tuning for 6000 RPM with a heavyweight," says Ulrich.

V-Thunder's Ben Kudon suggests that you also focus on how the cam may work with the rest of your engine package. "Everything has to be in balance," he says. "The carburetor, air filter, exhaust, camshaft, and ignition should all work together." If you have a big-inch engine with wide-open exhausts and a yawning carburetor, the engine will tolerate a much hotter cam. For most of us, with largely stock, 80-inch Big Twins, Kudon (and the others) once again recommends a mild cam.

So swallow hard and resist the temptation to buy a cam that makes your bike idle like a top-fuel dragster and has as much power in the usable (read: low) part of the powerband as a weed whacker. Make the right choice and you'll enjoy the delicious pleasure of blowing by Mr. Big Cam's bike in any roll-on contest.

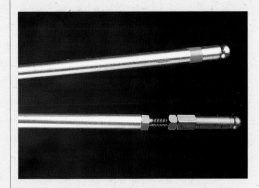

Adjustable pushrods—particularly those with long-travel threads—make cam work on Big Twins much easier. Once they're installed, you can change the cam or lifters without disturbing the rocker boxes. Standard solid pushrods are fine for most mild tuning applications, though. Moreover, adjustable pushrods buy you little on post-1991 Sportsters because of that bike's one-piece pushrod shrouds; you have to break into the rocker boxes any time you change cams, regardless of pushrod type.

Above and right: Cylinder head work often entails grinding out the ports and fitting larger valves. This is not a task for the uninitiated. In fact, for the vast majority of riders, the stock heads provide satisfying performance without the expense or risk of going into the engine.

time to move on to the next stage. This entails going with a more aggressive state of tune.

First among the changes should be a replacement camshaft or camshaft set. Stock Harley cams are quite mild, and the engine's state of tune benefits greatly from more aggressive grinds. Don't go overboard here—you're still dealing with a stock-displacement engine with standard ports and valves. There's only so much breathing room in that head, so you must choose appropriately. (See page 130: Choosing the Right Camshaft.)

Installing a cam is involved enough that you should let a good shop or your Harley dealer do the work. Plan on between four and six hours' labor. Although just about any decent shop will know enough to replace the standard inboard cam bearing on Evolution Big Twins, make a point to ask about the Torrington piece anyway. Harley's stock bearing has a poor service history with aftermarket cams.

Along with the cam job, you might get the hard sell on new rockers, pushrods, lifters, and all manner of high-end speed equipment. At this point, you should probably demur because they won't net you much performance. The only item on this list that might be of any help is a new set of pushrods, but only because some aftermarket units come with widely adjustable lengths that allow the installer to replace the cam without disturbing the rocker boxes. Moreover, using these adjustable pushrods will make future cam swaps much easier. Otherwise the stock components—lifters, pushrods, rockers, and other valvetrain bits—will be well up to the task of your project.

Advanced Exhaust and Carburetion

You might also want to consider upping the ante with a better-flowing carburetor and exhaust system—if you elected to keep the stock CV and, perhaps, just use slip-on mufflers for the first stage. But if you're happy with the way your bike sounds on the system you have, be sure to ride with it and the new cam for several hundred miles before changing it for another exhaust system.

This book is not intended to be the definitive discussion of Harley-engine hop-ups. Following are some of the logical steps to Stage 3 higher power that are described in high-performance tuning books.

A Word About Dyno Numbers

It's tempting to build an engine that will rip the dynamometer from its mounts with triple-digit figures—and some makers of aftermarket products will try to convince you that their products are the best based on impressive dyno figures.

Take a closer look at the numbers before you decide. And remember two things: Numbers can be made to lie, and, perhaps most importantly, you don't ride a motorcycle on a dyno. Numbers that look really impressive on the catalog page don't necessarily translate into an enjoyable bike.

How do you avoid the pitfalls? First, you should exclude from your consideration any power gains that appear mainly in the last 1000 or 1500 RPM of the powerband. Precious few riders ever twist their engines beyond 4500 RPM, and engines that make tire-melting power at the top end almost always sacrifice torque and drivability down low.

The dyno chart like the one at right shows the difference between the stock bike and one modified with an aftermarket kit. Notice how the numbers below 3000 RPM aren't shown. Also notice how the stock bike is actually stronger below 4000 RPM. Chances are this engine's tune would make for a less-than-enjoyable ride. Sure, there's lots of top-end power, and it's fairly broad across the top, but in real-world riding conditions, few riders will spin their engines fast enough, often enough, to take advantage of the increase. Meanwhile, they will have to live with a low end that's not as strong as stock.

Finally, many manufacturers use Dynojet dynamometers to determine power increases from their modifications. But the Dynojet is not a true dynamometer. Rather, it measures acceleration against a known mass and computes horsepower and torque from that figure. As such, this dyno is prone to calibration errors and is subject to operator technique. And while back-to-back numbers on the same dyno on the same day will reveal the true nature of any changes, it's folly to use the raw numbers from one manufacturer to compare the figures from another manufacturer's dyno.

Below: There's plenty of reserve power to be found in the modern Evolution engine. Simple intake and exhaust changes can open up the powerband significantly. Don't be surprised to see a stock-displacement Big Twin edge near 70 horsepower with comparatively minor changes. Notice, too, that you sometimes give up a bit of torque at the bottom end.

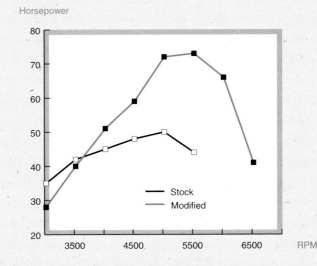

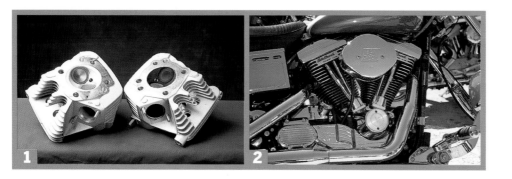

1. Harley's Screamin' Eagle division sells the Lightning heads for Sportsters (left). Compared with the stock 883 items (which have smaller combustion chambers and smaller valves than the standard 1200cc XLs), the Lightning heads are freer flowing, thanks to bigger ports and larger valves. They can use stock 1200 Sportster pistons for a 9.8:1 compression ratio; stock Sportsters (except for the dual-plug XL1200S) are 8.5:1.

2. This Dyna Glide has Edelbrock's high-flow cylinder heads, which need to be installed with proprietary Edelbrock pistons because the stock pistons will not work with the Edelbrock figure-eight combustion chamber. It also has an Edelbrock Qwiksilver carburetor and air-cleaner assembly. A Carlini torque arm ties the engine together on the side opposite the primary drive, to provide better overall chassis rigidity.

Stage 3 (and Beyond)

Beyond what's been discussed here, the next steps are usually:

- Cylinder-head modifications like porting, combustion-chamber reshaping, and racing-style valve jobs that include larger valves.

- Aftermarket cylinder heads, like those available from Custom Chrome (the RevTech line), Edelbrock, S&S, and (for Sportsters) Harley-Davidson's P&A division. Usually, these heads will have more aggressive porting and performance-oriented combustion chambers. A few, like the Edelbrock, will require proprietary intake manifolds as well. There are also a number of machined-from-billet cylinder heads on the market, including those from Johnson Racing, V-Thunder, and others.

- Using so-called stroker flywheels. By increasing the stroke of the Evolution Big Twin engine, you also increase displacement and thereby torque production greatly. Standard 1340cc/80-cubic-inch engines use cylinders with a 3 $\frac{1}{2}$ -inch bore and a 4 $\frac{1}{2}$ -inch stroke. A stroked engine with stock bore is extremely common. To get to 88 inches, stretch the stroke to 4 $\frac{5}{8}$ inches. Another common step is to also increase the bore size by $\frac{1}{8}$ inch, which, with a 4 $\frac{5}{8}$ -inch stroke will get you a 96-inch engine. (Additional increases in bore size are complicated by the fact that the narrow-angle vee makes it likely that the skirts of big-bore pistons will touch.) Natu-

rally, the strokers will need new flywheels and connecting rods, while the bored-out engines will also need new pistons and rings.

- There are also much bigger-displacement engines, but they require considerable crankcase machinations and also call for stronger driveline components like transmission gears and clutch.

The installation of any of these "advanced" components will greatly increase the complexity of your hop-up and, regardless of what you may have read in the advertisements, will reduce the reliability of your engine. (There's no getting around the simple fact, based in elementary physics, that an engine making more power is under greater mechanical and thermal stresses.)

In any event, the seasoned hot-rodders and engine gurus unanimously recommend that you start your engine modifications in the aforementioned sequence. This way, you'll have the benefit of seeing the gradual advances and avoid buying components twice. (If you buy a too-aggressive cam, for example, you may end up purchasing another, milder cam later on.) More to the point, you have the opportunity to increase both your bike's power and your monetary investment in it incrementally.

After you have unlocked your 75 or so horsepower—and, again, more important, your 80 foot-pounds of torque—you can then revel in the fact that your charismatic, historically significant engine also makes some serious horsepower. There's *nothing* better than horsepower.

Installing a Jet Kit

As backyard performance tweaks go, installing a jet kit is a pretty painless process. Start by having the replacement items ready—your jet kit, a new, freer-flowing air-cleaner assembly, and the appropriate crankcase breather kit. Installing a jet kit with the stock air cleaner nets you just a fraction of the potential benefits. Turn off the petcock and free the choke knob from the mounting tab by loosening the nut on the back; the mount is slotted so you can just let the knob-end fall free.

Remove the old air cleaner, taking care to note the location of the stock components. The single large Allen-head bolt secures the covers, while three smaller bolts hold the air-cleaner backing plate to the carburetor inlet flange and two hollow bolts at the inboard edges of the rocker boxes further secure the air cleaner and permit the crankcase to breathe through the stock air cleaner. Disconnect the electrical connections to the VOES solenoid and remove the air-cleaner backing plate.

While you could perform all the work with the carb on the bike, it's worth the effort to remove it and bring it to your bench. Remove the throttle cables by holding the throttle wide open against

the small spring at the ferrule-end of the return cable. Lift the pull cable from the ferrule and relax the throttle. The return cable will come out of the ferrule; you can remove both cable ends from the throttle bellcrank.

The Keihin CV carburetor is used in all post-1987 Big Twins and all Evolution Sportsters. In the pre-1990 models, the carb mounts to the manifold with a two-bolt flange; on more recent bikes, the carb is simply pressed into the rubber intake-manifold spigot and held in place by the air cleaner. Gently pull the carburetor from the spigot or unbolt the coupling.

Using a recalibration kits entails replacing one or more of the jets, the main-jet atomizer tube, the needle (swapping the stock, one-setting needle for one with adjustment notches), and the slide return spring (for one of a lighter spring rate for better throttle response). Read the directions provided with the jet kit carefully; some call for drilling out a bleed hole

1. Jet kits are at the heart of any performance upgrade for the Evolution engine. This is Dynojet's version, although the various brands are essentially interchangeable.

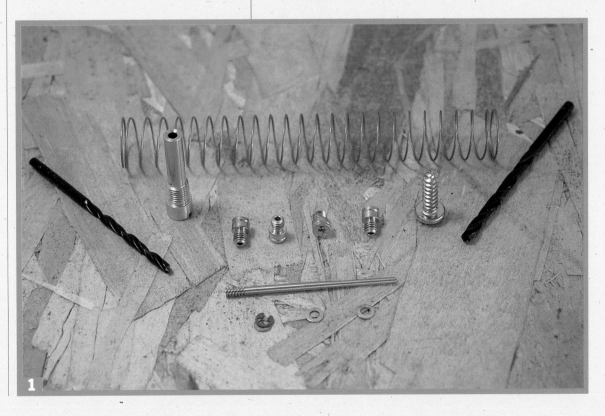

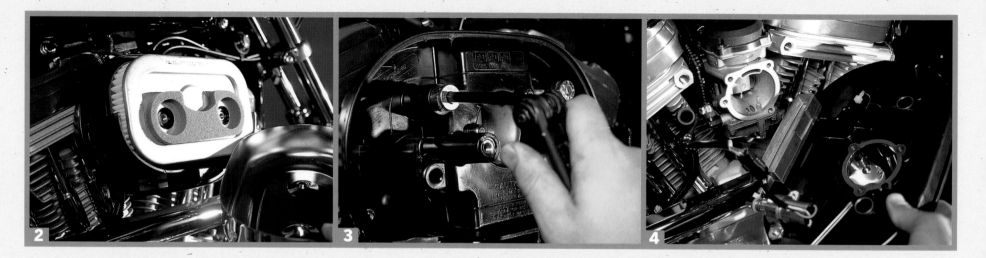

in the bottom of the slide to improve responsiveness. All the kits recommend a separate operation of drilling out the antitampering cover on the idle-mixture screw. Take extreme care in drilling out the cover to the idle-mixture screw. Overdrill and you'll destroy the soft brass head.

Remove the float bowl, being careful not to strip the heads of the small Phillips screws. Sometimes these are a real bear to extricate, so if your bike has more than a few thousand miles on it, you should apply penetrating oil and come back after lunch. Drop the float bowl and note the location of the main and pilot jets. Remove them. Bear in mind that these brass metering devices are soft, so use your tools carefully.

Install the new jets. Depending on the state of tune of the bike—that is,

which cam you may have installed and which exhaust system is in place—you will have to decide how much richer than stock to go. For a mild bike—particularly those with stock cams and slip-on mufflers—start at the baseline recommended by the kit maker and set the idle-mixture screw as stipulated.

Next you'll need to disassemble the slide and vacuum chamber at the top of the carb. Again, four small screws do the deed here. Remove the cover and lift the diaphragm/slide straight out of the carb body. Be careful not to nick or tear the rubber diaphragm. The needle protruding from the bottom of the slide is held in place by a small plastic cage. Remove it and drop the needle out the top. Note that it has no means of adjustment, while the replacement needle has five notches and a supplied circlip.

2. **First, remove the stock airbox cover and air filter.**
3. **Extricate the backing plate by removing the two breather bolts with an 8mm Allen wrench.**
4. **Disconnect the wires and hoses from the back side of the air-cleaner assembly; mark them if you're unsure whether you'll remember where they need to go later.**

Reassemble the top of the carb, being careful that the diaphragm's outer circumference fits in the small machined slot in the carburetor. Reinstall the carburetor and the air-cleaner assembly.

5. Cut the fuel-line clamp with diagonal cutters and be ready to catch the slight dribble of fuel that comes next. Slide the carb out of the spigot.

6. Remove the four screws holding down the diaphragm cover.

7. Carefully lift the diaphragm out and turn it upside down. A white plastic spring retainer will drop out, followed by the fixed needle.

8. Aftermarket jet kits come with adjustable needles. The small C-clip determines how far into the main jet this needle protrudes. Remember, raising the clip on the needle sends it farther into the main jet, thus leaning the mixture.

9. Remove the screws holding the float bowl onto the bottom of the carb. Use care with these screws because the heads strip out easily.

10. The main jet is attached to an emulsion tube. Some carb kits contain new tubes; use the method recommended by your jet-kit maker. The main jet rides atop the tube; be careful because the brass is soft.

11. The pilot jet lives in a small well next to the main jet. Its main function is to meter fuel between idle and about one-half throttle.

12. Idle mixture adjustment is made with this screw. You'll have to drill out a small blanking plate to gain access to it. Turning in the screw enriches the idle mixture.

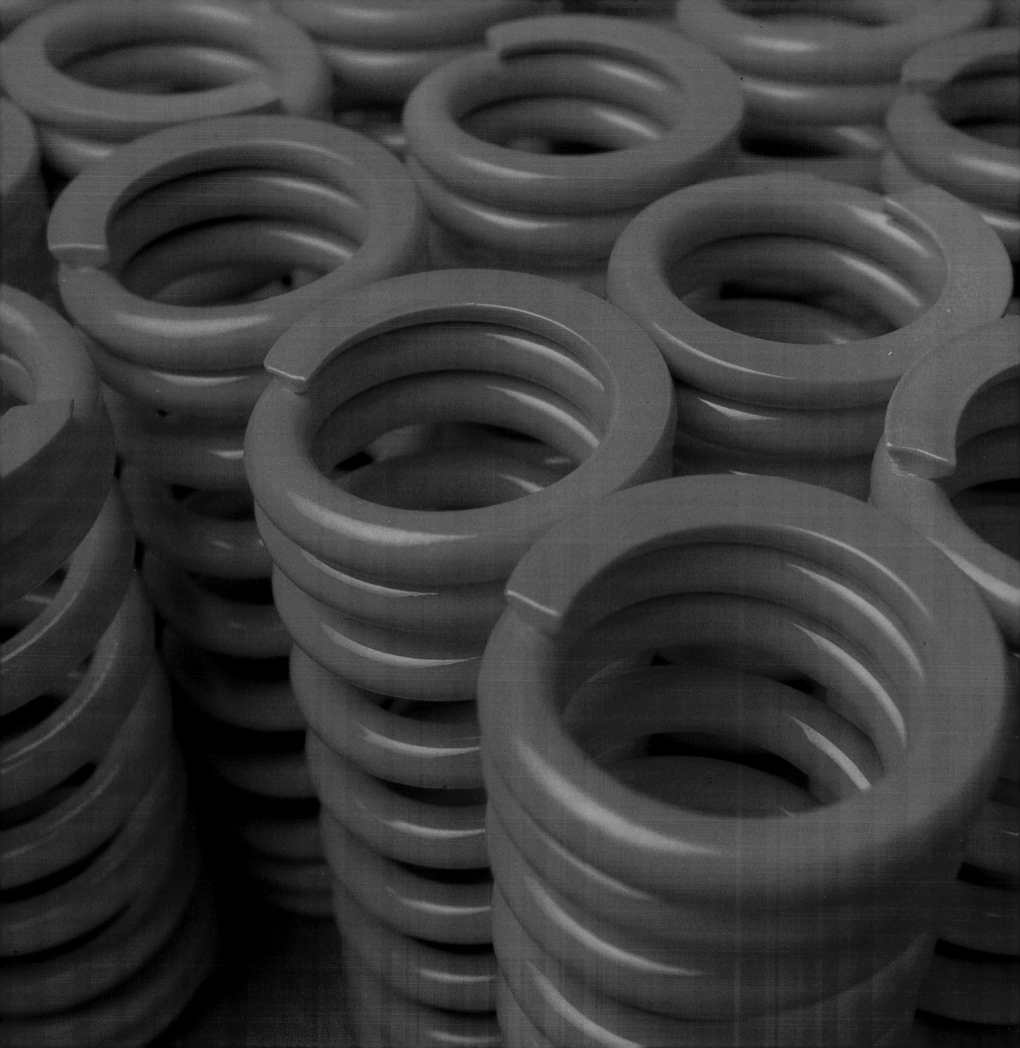

Chapter 6:

Suspension

In a perfect world, the tires would faithfully follow the contours of the road for optimum traction, while the chassis itself would sail along as though afloat on a cloud.

The point of suspension is to isolate the rider from jarring bumps and to respond at vastly different velocities to keep the tires in ideal contact with the road. In a perfect world, the tires would faithfully follow the contours of the road for optimum traction, while the chassis itself would sail along as though afloat on a cloud. Moreover, the ideal motorcycle's suspension would also not be so soft as to cause the bike to squat hard during acceleration or plunge to the fork's stops during spirited braking.

Opposite: Progressive Suspension's high volume means it buys springs by the barrel. Steel springs can be made in a bewildering range of rates and styles. As the name implies, Progressive prefers to build shocks and fork kits with progressive spring rates. This results in the greatest flexibility for a broad number of bikes.

Unfortunately, making it work well is not quite as elementary. Both wheels must be able to follow road irregularities big and small and should respond at vastly different velocities to keep the tires in ideal contact with the road. After all, a suspension that fails to follow the profile of the highway does nothing for the bike's ability to steer or put the power down.

Here's the Theory

Suspension terminology breaks down the basic functions of the system like this:

Springs carry the load of the motorcycle. The spring—whether it's in the shock or the fork—is nothing more complicated than a steel bar. Applying a load or force to the end of a bar deflects it a certain amount depending on its thickness, diameter, and hardness. A coil spring is essentially this steel rod wound around a common axis.

Above: Chrome fork components are common. This Softail-style fork uses steel gaiters to protect the otherwise exposed stanchions, a styling cue taken from Harley's first hydraulic fork models.

Left: Progressively wound fork springs—you can tell by the different pitch of the coils. As the spring compresses, the closely spaced coils touch each other (called coil binding), essentially locking out a section of the spring. As a result, the overall spring rate increases as the spring compresses.

Properly chosen, this spring should provide the correct ride height and ride quality. The suspension should not use most of its travel just holding up the bike and rider. Springs come in various lengths and rates—the higher the rate, the more the spring can carry before compressing.

It's a fine line between a spring that's so stiff you feel every little irregularity in the road and one that's so soft the bike sinks under its own weight and pitches like a drunken horse during acceleration and braking. Suspension designers spend many an hour on the computer, followed by extensive testing, before selecting spring rates. Moreover, bikes that experience a wide range of loads— like a touring rig—are even more difficult to tune well. The engineer must make the bike livable with just a lightweight rider aboard as well as for when the bike is loaded to the gunwales with on-the-road accouterments.

Spring rate is the resistance to movement by the spring. A 100 pound-per-inch spring simply means that if you stack 100 pounds on it, the spring will be 1 inch shorter than when you started. Sometimes, suspension makers specify dual, multiple, or progressive spring rates. A dual-rate setup employs springs of two different rates. In the suspension, the softer spring compresses first until it either bottoms out or coil binds and then the stiffer spring takes over. There are also multiple-rate setups that use a number of discrete springs to give different beginning, ending, and intermediate rates.

A progressive spring uses coils that are wound progressively tighter at one end. This way, when the spring compresses, the coils begin to bind progressively; as each coil binds, it effectively locks out that part of the spring and relies on the remainder of the spring to carry the load. The remaining spring is therefore of a higher rate than the whole spring uncompressed.

1-2. Harley has used a number of mud-wiper configurations over the years, including plain-looking rubber items as well as the handsome polished wipers used on the narrow-glide forks today. Here is a chrome cover that fits over the standard wiper. Some models of these covers come in two pieces, so you don't have to remove the fork from the bike to install them. They are, however, slightly less secure than the one-piece items.

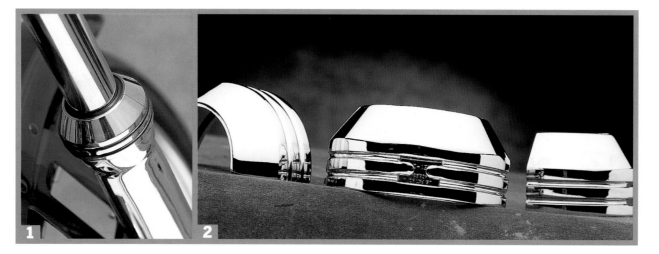

Above: Harley's Profile Low shocks are built by Fox Racing Shox. Available for Dyna, FXR, and XL models, the Profile Low shocks are recommended to be installed in conjunction with a fork-lowering kit.

Left: Polished lower fork legs look great against chrome gaiters.

Right: Some riders dislike seeing the mechanicals of the shock, so they use covered shocks, like these sold by Drag Specialties. For most riding, covering the shock, which limits the amount of cooling air available to the shock body, is not a problem.

Left: This is the Wide Glide fork. On stock Harleys, this means fork legs separated by wider triple clamps. Also, for the original Harley bits, it means a larger-diameter fork, 41mm versus 39mm on the other narrow-glide front ends.

Spring preload defines how much the spring is compressed with the suspension at full extension. Preload helps to set the initial spring rate and ride height. For example, if you have a 100-pound/inch spring and it's preloaded by one inch, that shock will need to be compressed with 200 pounds of force to move the first inch. After that, the shock will deflect an inch for every additional 100 pounds presented to it.

Springs are great for absorbing bumps. They soak up and store the energy from the bike's movement over a bump. The big problem with springs is that after absorbing that energy they want to bounce back at the same rate they were compressed.

That's where *dampers* come in. Dampers, also called shocks, though this term most often applies to combination spring/damper units, use hydraulics to prevent the spring from returning all its energy to the wheel at once. In the most basic terms, shocks contain a sealed cylinder filled with oil that itself contains a simple piston with variously sized holes. As the piston, which is on a shaft that connects it between the frame and wheel, tries to move, the oil resists the movement. The thickness of the oil, the number and placement of damping holes, and various other factors determine how forcefully the damper will resist movement of the wheel and in which direction of wheel travel that resistance takes place.

These movements are called *compression* when the wheel is moving up its line of travel and *rebound* when the wheel is moving back against the road. Some shocks and a few fork models for Harleys have adjustable damping rates; most are adjustable for rebound damping, while a few others also have compression-damping adjustments.

A few more terms: Damping terminology can be further divided into high-speed and low-speed. This has nothing to do with the speed of the motorcycle, but rather the velocity of the suspension/wheel itself. High-speed movements take place over small, sharp bumps, like frost heaves or the segments on concrete highways. Low-speed damping comes into play during braking and acceleration, when the suspension takes high loads but reacts slowly. There are, of course, interactions, such as when you hit a series of small stutter bumps while also on the brakes; in this case, the suspension must absorb both the long-term loads from braking and the short-term movements from the bumps.

A suspension that can isolate the small bumps without also allowing the bike to pitch and wallow excessively is considered ideal.

Left: Polishing the lower fork legs is a popular modification. It requires complete disassembly of the fork and meticulous cleaning before reassembly to make sure no foreign matter is left behind. The inside of any fork is a high-pressure hydraulic system, so any abrasive matter will chew through seals in no time. Standard finish is a matte polish with clearcoat.

1. **Good suspension manufacturers use something called a shock dyno to test and develop new suspension technology. This dyno, at Progressive Suspension, can measure the damping forces at various shock speeds and plot them on a chart.**

2. **Most Harley shocks provide adjustment only for spring preload, thanks to a ramped collar. Turning the collar increases the compression of the spring (it is already slightly compressed when installed on the shock body), which helps set the static ride height of the bike and compensate for varying passenger loads.**

Opposite: **Harley's narrowglide front fork on an FXR. The components have been highly polished. Harley switched to a 39mm fork in 1987, up from a very old 35mm design. The larger touring rigs have 41mm fork tubes.**

About Harley Suspension Tuning

A number of considerations determine how well any suspension system works, and it's worth noting that Harleys have the deck stacked against them in several ways. For starters, Harleys are generally heavy motorcycles. But the more massive the body, the more difficult it is to reach an ideal compromise between settings that will allow smooth movement of the wheels over small pavement blotches while still retaining enough spring rate and damping to prevent the wheels from bottoming out.

Harley wheels also tend to be quite heavy. Ideally, you'd have the lightest wheel possible—to reduce what's called *unsprung weight*. A lighter wheel can follow the road more accurately than a heavy one.

Finally, many Harley models have comparatively kicked-out steering-head angles. Such an obtuse angle makes road jolts try to bend the fork as much as compress it, so it's very difficult to get both a supple ride and good resistance to bottoming. The best you can hope for with, say, 32-degree models is to set the spring rates as light as you dare for a good ride over the small stuff, and make the spring and damping rates highly progressive. That is, the rates are not linear through the fork's travel but increase dramatically at the end. In this way, the fork can be reasonably compliant without slamming to the stops when you brake hard. Such a dilemma is why Harley fits the FL models with an unusual steering-head arrangement: The fork tubes and steering head are at a very steep, 26-degree angle, but because the fork stanchions are

Below: By far the most straightforward way to lower the rear of the bike—if not the least expensive—is to buy a shorter replacement shock. This Sportster has shorter-than-stock shocks that help reduce seat height. A main advantage is that shorter shocks also have less travel, so the wheel ends up penetrating no farther into the fender than with the original suspension.

"Regardless of what you may read in the catalogs, a short-travel suspension cannot—will not—be as supple and comfortable as one with more travel."

behind the steering head, the bike has a lot of trail. Trail helps improve a bike's self-centering tendencies and thereby increases stability.

The Stock Equipment

Harley contracts to Showa of Japan for suspension components and, as you might expect, is quite cost-conscious. As a result, the parts Harley buys are manufactured to a budget and relatively basic in their technology, having more in common with components of early 1980s design than contemporary technology. Harley does offer adjustable suspension on the touring rigs and Sportster Sport, but conventional damping-rod forks are the norm, and the vast majority of the shocks fitted have no adjustment other than spring preload.

The Lowdown on Lowering

Many Harley riders want their bikes to be low, low, low. No problem with that stylistically—in fact, there's no denying that a long, low Harley is a sight to behold—but such a request proves a difficult challenge for the suspension engineers because the more travel you have available, the softer you can make the spring and damping rates. This allows the movement of the suspension to absorb the energy of an impact through travel.

But the short-travel suspension required to lower a bike prevents this style of tuning, and requires generally higher spring rates and, in particular, much higher compression-damping rates. The main reason stock Harleys seem to ride rough over sharp-edged bumps like concrete expansion joints

is that the factory tuning favors lots of compression damping over stout springs. In the grand scheme of things, it's much easier to make long-travel suspension work well with few compromises. Start hacking into that travel, and the compromises will become considerably greater.

So should you decide to lower your bike, keep these caveats in mind. First, regardless of what you may read in the catalogs, a short-travel suspension cannot—will not—be as supple and comfortable as one with more travel. At least it can't without sacrificing something, like the ability to absorb large thumps without bottoming out. Second, lowering your motorcycle will, in some cases, dramatically reduce cornering clearance. Say you're not a canyon racer so it's not a big deal? Well, a few radically lowered bikes negotiate turns at a pace that would have school buses hounding the taillight and are unable to make it past a moderately crowned driveway without leaving some paint behind.

Also, it may be possible that your sidestand—or Jiffy stand, in Harley parlance—will no longer keep the bike properly upright. Harley sells a shorter sidestand as part of its lowering kits, and you can also buy the stands designed for the short-travel bikes (XLH Hugger, 1200 Custom, Dyna Low Rider, etc.). Finally, understand that lowering the back of the motorcycle compromises the bike's handling under extreme acceleration. If an imaginary line from the rear axle to the countershaft centerline passes above the swingarm pivot—which it almost certainly will if you've lowered the back end much—the bike will be prone to rear-

Softails Are Special

Because of the design elements involved in hiding the Softails' twin shocks under the transmission, this model suffers even more in lowering the suspension. A very high leverage ratio—about six to one—between the rear wheel and the shocks means that suspension designers have relatively little shock movement to work with.

Despite these considerations, Softails are perhaps the most often lowered models in the lineup. A couple of aftermarket companies provide alternative suspension setups—one makes a torsion bar that uses a modified swingarm pivot in lieu of the normal coil-over springs, and another uses a leaf spring pressed against the swingarm's upper crossover member.

So, How Do I Lower the Bike?

There are several methods to achieving that in-the-weeds ride. The most effective overall is to buy shorter suspension components. Harley's P&A division offers basic suspension packages for the long-travel bikes that duplicates what the company puts on the short-leg models. This includes shorter shocks—shorter both in overall length as well as in travel—and shorter fork tubes.

Reproducing the stock setup from the short-travel bikes is fine for casual riders, but many of the more aggressive and, for lack of a better term, nitpicky types, prefer to upgrade to a different type of suspension.

Because it's relatively easy to produce shock absorbers, and also because many of the Harley mod-

Softails are lowered perhaps more than any other of Harley's models because they look so good as a result. The long, low frame helps create that "sucked to the ground" look.

wheel squat during acceleration. This consumes wheel travel under conditions when you need as much as you can get.

All shocks designed to shorten the ride height will have less travel and, generally, be firmer and harsher-riding than stock-length shocks.

Extreme care must be taken when reducing the ride height without also reducing shock and wheel travel. It's possible that lowered suspension will allow tire-to-fender contact, which does nothing good for the ride of the bike, nor the life of the tire. This is a serious concern.

Below: The visual results of lowering the bike, or "slamming" it. The wheels appear to be sucked into the fenders, and the chassis seems to be skimming along just inches above the ground. This is the look many riders want.

els use the same or similar shocks, there's a plethora of shocks in the aftermarket. They range in capability and price from modest upgrades with fixed damping to all-out racing shocks that can set you back $1000 for the pair.

Harley P&A has developed a business relationship with Fox Racing Shox to sell this company's wares as the Profile Low Suspension. Available for Dynas, FXRs, and Sportsters, this version of the Profile shock lowers the bike by about an inch at the rear, while providing better and more progressive damping than the stock shock. Harley has also teamed with Showa to produce special versions of the Softail and FL-series shocks that result in about an inch lower ride height.

Finally, Harley will be happy to sell XL owners the same Showa shocks fitted to the XL1200S Sportster Sport—complete with rebound and compression adjustments. These OEM bits are as expensive as the high-end aftermarket parts.

Model	Standard shock length (in inches)
FXR, FXRS, FXRT	13
FXR Low Rider	12 1/2
FXRS-SP	13 5/8
Dyna Glide	12 1/2
Dyna Low Rider	11 1/2
FLT, FLHS	13
XL 883, 1200	13 5/8
XL 883 Hugger, 1200C ('91 and later)	11 3/4
XL 883 Hugger ('87 to '90)	12 1/2

For reference, a chart listing the standard shock lengths for recent Harley models. Use this when comparing the stated lengths of aftermarket shocks.

A Progressive Approach

Progressive Suspension has built something of an empire on the Harley aftermarket, in part because it provides a broad range of H-D applications. Progressive takes an interesting approach to supplying the Harley market, too. Because of the design of the shocks and fork kits, the company believes it can follow, essentially, a one-size-fits-all approach. As a result, you will see the same part-number shock for both a Sportster and an FXR, even though the bikes are considerably different in weight. Part of Progressive's thinking is a result of its progressive-rate springs—for both the shocks and fork—that accommodate riders and bikes in a relatively wide range of weights and riding styles. Even so, riders of particularly heavy or light bikes

Right: Progressive Suspension's 418-series aluminum body shocks provide five-way adjustable rebound damping. Changing the rebound damping characteristics allows you to compensate for increased spring preload or aggressive riding. Rebound damping controls the rate at which the shock extends after being compressed by a bump.

Above: The main members of the Progressive line, left to right. Softail shock, 412, covered 412, and adjustable 418. Progressive builds on a one-size-fits-all philosophy: One range of damping rates is used for a given shock length, whether it's slated for a Dyna Glide or a Sportster. This tactic works surprisingly well for the vast majority of riders.

might find the law of averages excludes them from having the ideal ride.

Progressive's basic shock, the 412, uses fixed damping, a steel damper body, and progressively wound springs. It's available for almost every Harley, and in a wide range of lengths, from 11 inches to 14. With that range, you can easily tailor the rear ride height of your bike simply by choosing a different-length shock. Because not all the lengths have reduced shock-shaft travel to go along with their shorter total length, you must be cautious of substituting a shock that's more than about an inch shorter than stock. You can also order the 412 with black or chrome springs. Progressive's design philosophy results in a surprisingly economical shock.

Next up the ladder is Progressive's 418 shock. It uses a steel inner body with an aluminum outer skin and comes with five-way rebound-damping adjustment as well as a four-position spring preload mechanism. Again, the shocks are available in lengths from 11 ½ to 13 ½ inches

Progressive also makes air-spring shocks. Harley touring models come standard with air shocks, mainly because this type allows for a greater range of loads than a conventional spring shock. However, at high air-pressure settings, these shocks can provide a harsher ride than a properly rated coil setup. That's because air as a springing medium is very progressive, with a fairly light rate early in the travel (or at low initial pressures) and a dramatic increase in spring rate near bottoming. The greater the initial pressure, the steeper this

progression. Air shocks also use standard coil springs that set the minimum rate and use the air as an assist for greater loads. Progressive's 416 air shock has, like the stock Harley model, fixed damping.

Finally, there's Progressive's 413 shock for Softails. Recently, Progressive made these shocks available with adjustable eye lengths so that you can tailor the ride height of your Softail. Naturally, the 413 has progressive-rate springs and more aggressive damping than the stock item.

Works Performance

If going the route of Progressive Suspension is akin to buying a suit off the rack, then Works Performance is more like a custom-tailored approach. Every shock ordered from Works is made to order. Put the money down at your dealer and you'll be handed a form asking for, among other things, bike model, rider weight, likely use of passengers,

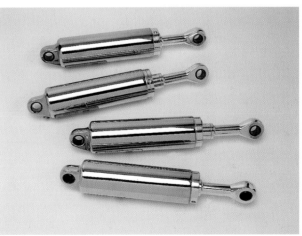

Opposite: An important caveat: Softails don't have much suspension travel to begin with; lowering will consume a significant portion of it and render the ride choppier than before.

Left: Works Performance's Softail shocks use a thicker damping rod and more sophisticated damping controls than the original item. They are available in stock and lowered lengths; the longer the shock in a Softail, the lower the rear end of the bike.

Works Performance Street Trackers with black springs and chrome bodies in place on an FXR. Spring preload is adjustable; the small Schrader valve visible near the top shock eye is for adding a nitrogen charge during servicing. These are close to the stock length.

Left: Works Performance Street Trackers use a check-ball-style damping mechanism that is highly progressive. The shocks can be fitted with single- or dual-rate springs in black or chrome; they offer a plusher initial ride with good resistance to bottoming under heavy loads or over tall bumps.

Below: Works also has a clever ride-height-adjustable Softail shock that hydraulically changes the spring position on one of the two shocks. This way you can have the long, low look for cruising around town but also a decent amount of wheel travel for highway use.

riding style, and desired raising or lowering of the ride height. Then a single employee at Works analyzes the information and picks spring and damping rates for your shocks—it's done by one man to ensure long-term consistency in spring and damping choices. Three to seven days later, your shocks are on the way to your dealer.

Works' product line centers on the Street Tracker design. This single-tube shock is unique in that it uses small check balls and carefully selected orifices to manage most of the damping chores. (The more common way shocks operate is to use deflecting disks to control rebound and compression damping forces. The Works design has a small disk on the rebound side, but it's job is primarily to seal off the rebound side of the damper assembly.)

The basic Works design comes in your choice of steel (Steel Tracker), chromed steel (Chrome Tracker), or aluminum (Street Tracker) bodies; regardless, the internals are the same. All in this line of Trackers have fixed damping rates. Works offers the Trackers with several spring options, including chrome or black finish and single- or dual-rate springs. Also available is Works' ARS, or adjustable-rate suspension system. Using a mechanical stop, the ARS changes the way the shock transitions from the softer of the two springs to the harder. This allows you to adjust the overall spring rate as well as the transition point independently of preload. This ARS system is available with either cast or billet adjusting

cups; billet appearance cups can be purchased for other models in the Tracker line.

As with most other multimodel shock makers, Works will build your shocks to the length and travel you require. By juggling spring lengths and internal spacers, Works can create just about any combination of length and travel.

Works also builds an innovative Softail shock. By using hydraulic fluid to vary the beginning extension point, which defines the maximum wheel extension on a Softail, the Works adjustable ride-height shock gives riders the option of reducing overall ride height by as much as 1 1/2 inches. Because the hydraulic adjustment also increases

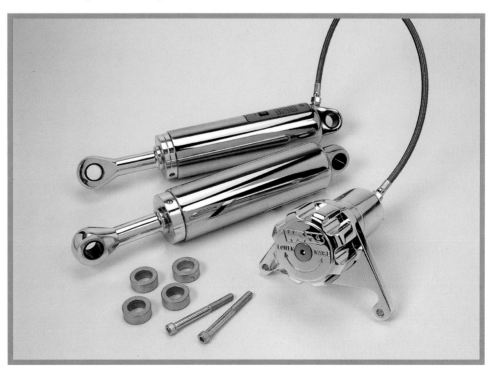

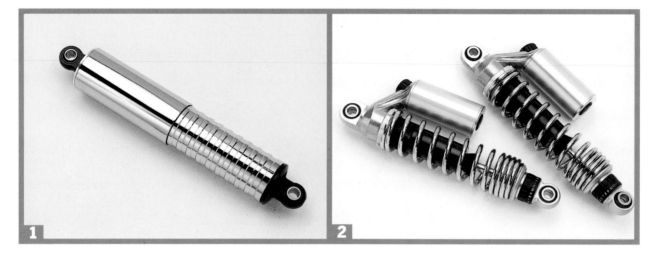

spring preload, the overall spring rate increases for the lowered suspension, as is desirable. For reasons of simplicity, only one of the adjustable shocks contains the ride-height mechanism; the other is a conventional Works Softail shock. A large adjuster wheel mounts to a frame tube or to the primary case. Cranking down on the adjuster lowers the bike.

Naturally, Works also sells a version of this shock without the ride-height adjuster; with different-length eye shanks, you can have an aftermarket shock with stock travel or one that lowers the bike by about an inch.

Works shocks are not the cheapest in the industry, nor does the order-and-wait scenario accommodate instant gratification, but many riders like the idea of a custom-made shock, one tailored for a specific bike and rider and riding style.

1. **Air shocks use high-pressure air as part of the spring medium. Delta Fournales shocks rely on adjustable air bladders for spring preload and ride height.**

2. **Highly adjustable WP Twin Adjuster shocks, sold by White Brothers in the U.S., are available in a number of lengths and include compression and rebound damping adjustments. These shocks have progressively wound springs. They are high-end items and are priced accordingly.**

Other Shock Builders

White Brothers imports the WP line of suspension components from Holland; this European manufacturer is highly regarded in racing circles. For Harleys, White Brothers has the WP Super Adjuster shocks. This modern design has both rebound and compression damping adjustments as well as adjustable spring preload and optional chrome spring cups. However, because these shocks have rather large external fluid/nitrogen reservoirs, you have to be sure the bike has sufficient clearance between the swingarm, shock, and frame. They aren't cheap.

Above: **One way to lower without buying new shocks is to use a lowering kit. This White Brothers kit simply moves the lower shock eyes farther along the swingarm, reducing travel even while using the stock shocks. Because the amount of travel is the same, you must be careful that the tire will not bottom on the fender or fender hardware before reaching the limit of travel.**

Also, as is true of a lot of other aftermarket shocks, it's possible that you will have to carve out some of the belt guard or fender to make room for the bottom spring cups, which are larger than the stock shocks'. Some other bikes, later Sportsters in particular, may need a spacer washer to move the lower attach points away from the belt guard.

White Brothers also distributes the J. P. Fournales air shocks, both for Softails and conventional, twin-shock models. These shocks provide some measure of ride-height adjustment and a pronounced progression curve to the spring rate because of the air assist. They are also priced like premium product.

Lowering without Buying New Shocks

White Brothers has developed several innovative products that allow for lowering the rear of the bike while still using the stock shocks. One of the

Above: **White Brothers' lowering kit for Softail shocks simply extends the mounting eye, which lengthens the shock and lowers the rear end of the bike. Adjustable turnbuckles allow you to set the ride height you want. Remember, though, that the total travel is not changed, so use care to check that the tire does not contact the chassis at full bump.**

For some models, Harley made the Springer components in black. Many customizers have taken the stock chrome units, stripped them, and painted them to match whatever scheme they have in mind. There's no limit on what you can do visually with these parts.

company's lowering kits is deceptively simple: A steel bracket relocates the lower shock mount rearward sufficiently to lower the back of the bike an inch or two. These lowering kits are available for most models of Sportster, Dyna Glide, FLH/FLT series, and FXR.

White Brothers was also the first with an elegant way to lower Softails—in fact, it has three ways to coerce the stock Softail shock to put the fender in the grass. By making a threaded shock eye that's longer than stock—remember that the Softail shock extends as the rear wheel goes up—the Lowboy lowering kit manages to drop the rear end by 1 $\frac{1}{2}$ inches, while still maintaining spring-preload adjustments. The company also sells an economy version that is simply a set of washers to insert between the standard shock eye and the shock itself. Finally, White Brothers has what it calls Adjust-A-Ride kits; these are replacement shock eyes that contain integral threaded adjustments. According to the company, this kit allows you to reduce ride height by as much as 1 $\frac{1}{2}$ inches, or increase it by $\frac{1}{2}$ inch.

Fork Reform

Harley's stock forks for the 1987-and-later bikes are built by Showa and come in 39mm and 41mm sizes, depending upon model. These are workmanlike, damping-rod-style suspenders that perform adequately for most applications. However, Harley tends to err on the side of low spring rates and light damping. This, combined with the nature of the damping-rod fork, tends to make most

Custom-crazed riders love
the Springer fork because
the mechanical bits are all
on the outside, ready to
be chromed, showed off,
and admired. In truth, the
Springer front end is not
quite as supple as a con-
ventional fork, but for
many riders, the look is
more than worth the
trade-off.

Race Tech Cartridge Emulators

Suspension technology moves fast. Particularly in off-road and roadracing circles, what was yesterday's hot setup is tomorrow's ancient history. Forks and shocks on dirt bikes display more adjustment knobs than an antique-radio convention, and the suspensions' internals employ current-think deflecting-disk damper mechanisms that can be tailored to respond just about any way the designer wishes.

But Harley suspension is comparatively basic. Save for the adjustable components on the Sportster XL1200S Sport, most of the current (and recent) Harleys use suspension pieces with limited adjustability and tunability. This is most notably true at the fork. High-tech street bikes and racers use what are called cartridge damper assemblies—a stack of steel shims that cover various damping orifices and are submerged in the fork oil. By altering the number and thickness of these shims, the damping qualities can be set to a very fine degree. For example, it's possible to increase the low-speed compression damping—as in the way the fork would resist diving during a hard stop—without influencing high-speed compression damping—that's the fork's resistance to small, rapid movements

like you'd feel over concrete-highway expansion joints.

It's important to understand that the conventional, damper-rod construction of most Harley forks is incapable, due to the limitations of the design, of such fine-tuning possibilities. Add thicker oil, for instance, and you'll get increased rebound damping, but also much more high- and low-speed compression damping. Moreover, because the

damper-rod fork uses oil flowing through plain holes, it's limited by the laws of fluid dynamics—in short, when the velocity of the fluid gets to a certain point, its resistance to being pushed through a hole increases dramatically. What you feel is a fork that will flop onto its stops during hard braking—because the low-speed compression damping is necessarily light—but will also deliver a jarring ride over cobblestone-like surfaces.

Race Tech, a suspension-tuning company in Pomona, California, has an answer to the damper-rod blues—the

The Race Tech Cartridge Emulator fits into the stock Harley fork and takes over all damping duties. Its deflecting-disk design makes the stock fork more tunable and allows you to adjust for high- and low-speed compression damping. This makes it possible to tune for a supple freeway ride yet retain good resistance to bottoming over large bumps.

Cartridge Emulator. This plainly clever device slips into a conventional fork and does a commendable job of providing the major benefits of cartridge-style damper systems at a fraction of the cost. The emulator fits over the open end of the damper rod, sandwiched between the top of the rod and the bottom of the fork spring. You must drill out the normal compression-damping holes near the bottom of the damping rod. The emulator takes over all the damping duties, so these large holes are needed to provide sufficient oil flow for the emulator to do its work. You also have the option of brazing closed some or all of the rebound-damping holes—these are the pin-size orifices near the head of the damper rod. If you're already performing fork maintenance that entails gaining access to the damping rod, installing emulators will add about thirty minutes to the job.

Better yet, the emulators perform as advertised. Typically, the revised Harley fork offers much less resistance to small bumps while preserving its ability to resist dive under braking. Moreover, the emulator allows you to increase the rebound damping—either by brazing the rebound hole closed or by increasing the viscosity of the damping oil—without sacrificing suppleness. Race Tech's emulator also affords some simple adjustments, although to make

them you have to gain access to the emulator itself. The spring holding closed the compressing-damping valve can be adjusted to change the rate at which the valve opens to relieve high-speed damping. Low-speed compression damping can also be altered by changing to a different fork oil.

Considering the benefits—a better, more controlled ride, some adjustability—the $125 Race Tech emulators are well worth the outlay, especially when you consider they're tremendously less expensive than stepping up to a high-tech replacement fork.

Paul Thede is the man behind Race Tech. He runs a rapidly growing suspension-tuning shop and gives seminars on the art and science of suspension tuning and rebuilding.

Harley forks a bit harsh over small bumps but also prone to bottoming during hard braking. Most riders prefer a slightly firmer ride than the stock bike provides, and a simple fork-spring change will make all the difference.

Progressive, true to its name, offers progressively wound springs for all the popular Harleys. For most applications, the Progressive fork spring requires the use of a small spacer to fit properly. This gives you some additional options compared with using the stock springs. That's because the standard Harley fork has no spacers and uses a slight amount of spring preload; you can increase the preload by adding spacers, but you cannot reduce it. On the other hand, with the Progressive spring—or any other spring product that uses spacers—you can tailor the spring preload by fitting spacers of different lengths. (Tuning by changing spring preload is a powerful tool, as you'll see in "Setting Up Your Suspension, page 166.")

Replacement springs are also available from Works Performance. As with its shocks, Works has a slightly different take on tuning. Its kits include two single-rate springs that, when used together, provide a dual-rate setup. But Works uses a trick similar to its ARS for the shocks. A series of small spacers that fit *inside* the softer spring help set the transition point from soft to hard. Although this adjustment is not accessible outside the fork, most riders find that the factory's baseline settings are just about right.

Lowering the Fork

Lowering the front of the bike is actually easier than reducing the height at the rear because you can probably use most of the stock components. Both Progressive and White Brothers sell lowering kits that replace the standard main spring with a shorter unit and substitute a longer rebound spring. (The rebound spring resides between the bottom of the damping-rod head and the bottom of the fork tube. It prevents the fork from topping out with a *thunk*.) This modification simply alters the topping-out point of the fork and makes it ride lower in its overall travel. The beauty of this modification is that it's entirely reversible—you can put the stock springs back in or remove the longer rebound spring easily and be back to the standard setup.

Harley sells a couple of different fork-lowering kits; one is a reduced-length main spring, while the other is essentially a complete replacement for most of the fork assembly. As with some of Harley's

The inverted fork is a styling trick taken from today's sportbikes. You must take care to make sure the triple clamps have similar offset to the original items and that the overall length of the fork is relatively close. Unless installed with care, high-zoot forks can look better than they work.

other kits, this more involved version uses many of the components on the factory-lowered suspension, including shorter sidestand.

Damping of the stock Harley fork can be altered by changing oil, modifying the stock damping rod, or purchasing a replacement rod from Progressive. Progressive's unit has smaller rebound-damping holes for increased resistance to topping out and slightly larger compression holes to help reduce the stocker's harshness. You can perform surgery on the stock damping rod—braze closed the small rebound holes near the top of the rod and redrill with orifices about half the size—or go to something more sophisticated like Race Tech's Cartridge Emulator. (See page 160 "Race Tech Cartridge Emulators.")

For lowered bikes, it's recommended to run Harley's heavier fork oil. You might also experiment with using slightly more oil than is called for in your service manual; add an extra ounce at a time and see how the fork works. The additional oil displaces some of the air in the fork, making the overall spring rate much more stiff and progressive near the end of travel. Use caution with this approach because too much oil will hydraulic-lock the fork at full compression and blow out the fork seals.

A Whole New Fork

It's possible to completely replace the fork with an aftermarket unit, in some cases with trick, high-tech inverted models. Is this your average, shadetree-mechanic kind of swap? Not really. You must be certain that the replacement fork is the

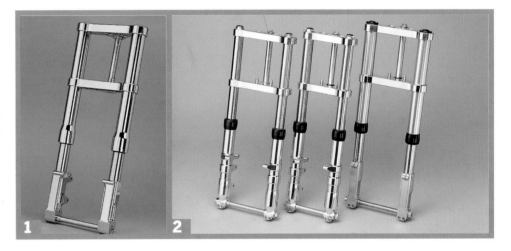

same (or nearly the same) length as the stocker, that the triple clamps provide the same geometry, and that all the brake and fender hardware will fit. Swapping your standard Harley fork for an aftermarket unit is far more involved than many riders initially think—and expensive, too. You will spend about ten times more replacing the fork than you would applying all the standard improvements to the stocker.

A notable exception is the replacement fork offered by Harley that's the same as the one used on the XL1200S. Because it slides into the stock triple clamps and has exactly the same geometry as the other long-travel Sportster forks, it's a straightforward swap. It is not inexpensive, though. But you do get a modern cartridge-style fork and external adjustments galore. For hard-core Sporty riders, this is a good, albeit expensive, alternative to tweaking the original fork.

1. This is the new Storz Performance inverted fork built in the U.S. from an Enrico Ceriani design. It uses 45mm sliders and massive 54mm upper legs. Inverted forks are generally stiffer than conventional units. But there's no denying the up-side-down fork has the look.

2. Storz Performance imports three models of the Ceriani fork. The standard models use 43mm stanchion tubes and cartridge dampers—the sophisticated cartridge damper systems are used by Harley only in the Sportster Sport—while the inverted, male-slider versions use 54mm stanchions.

Setting Up Your Suspension

Proper setup is as important as purchasing good suspension equipment. Even the best components, if poorly matched to the bike, will not perform well. For this exercise, you'll need some way to jack the bike—either both wheels simultaneously or one at a time—and a helper.

The first step is to set the spring preload—assuming you've already chosen your basic spring rates. First, jack the bike to fully extend the suspension. You're going to measure the extended free length of each end. Measure along the fork leg up front and from the shock eye or rear axle to some convenient point on the rear fender rail. (It doesn't really matter where this point is, as long as you use the same location for all measurements.)

Remove the jacks, mount the bike, and allow the suspension to compress normally. Have your assistant balance the bike while you assume the normal riding position. While doing so, have your assistant compress the suspension and slowly release; gently put your feet down just enough to support the bike. One of you notice if the suspension moves when you do this—if it doesn't, and it probably won't, then have your assistant take a measurement of the suspension sag. Next, have your assistant pull the suspension up—either by tugging on the fender or pushing up on the triple clamps—and let it down slowly. Take another measurement. (They should be very close; if they're different, take an average of the two.)

The difference between the ride height with the suspension topped out and with the rider aboard is called loaded sag or, sometimes, race sag. This is an important number. It should

1. **Check the rear suspension travel against some consistent marking point like the rear fender rail. First determine the unladen length of the rear suspension.**

2. **Next determine how much the bike sags under your weight. Total sag should be between one-fourth and one-third of the total travel. Less and the spring's too stiff—as is obvious here. More, you should increase spring preload or get shocks with stiffer springs.**

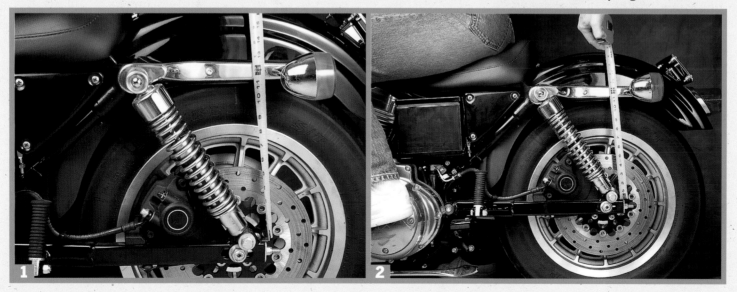

3. Measure the fork travel the same way, but do so along the length of the fork tubes. First take the unladen measurement with the bike jacked up so the suspension tops out.

4. With the rider aboard, check the laden sag. You can measure the total travel of the fork by placing a zip-tie around the stanchion tube and intentionally bottoming the suspension on a large bump. Alternatively, you can remove one of the fork caps, extract the spring, and let the suspension compress under the bike's weight. Again, you want between one-fourth and one-third of the suspension's travel to be consumed by the weight of the bike and rider.

be between 25 percent and 33 percent of the total suspension travel. Typically, the bikes with standard-length suspension have 4 1/2 to 5 inches of travel up front and 3 1/2 to 4 inches at the rear; short-travel bikes have 3 to 3 1/2 inches up front and 2 to 2 1/2 inches at the rear.

Set your spring preload according to this ratio of unladen to laden sag. If your bike has much less than 25 percent sag with the spring preload at its minimum, the spring rate is too stiff. If the bike compresses more than one-third of the travel even on the highest preload setting, the rate is too light. (Stock Harleys tend to swing in this direction.)

If you have an aftermarket set of fork springs, you can set the preload by using spacers inserted above the springs, below the fork caps. Most suspension suppliers specify a starting point for preload; chances are you won't need much, because the aftermarket rates tend to be substantially higher than you get from the factory.

It's important to get the sag settings right—if they're off, any other tuning you might attempt will lead to frustration.

Some aftermarket shocks come with adjustable rebound damping. Start in the middle of the range and ride the bike as you normally do. If the bike tends to kick back over large, sharp-

edged bumps, try the next-higher setting. If the bike "packs down" over a series of bumps, try the next-lower setting. As always, make one change at a time and test. Never make both a damping and spring (rate or preload) change at once.

Chapter 7:

Wheels & Brakes

Wheel choices are almost staggering. There are cast aluminum, billet aluminum, hybrids, wheels made from sheet material, and, of course, the ever-durable spoke wheel.

Call it a recent phenomenon. The use of wheels as decorative items on Harleys is a contemporary occurrence. In the early days, there were spokes: bicycle-style wheels with thin rims, high-pressure tube tires—and spokes. Perhaps as a testament to the quality of the spoke-wheel design, there were no alternatives on Harleys until the late 1970s, when the so-called mag wheel made inroads. (Mag, of course, refers to the racing-inspired magnesium wheels, even though most road-going versions were cast aluminum.) Fast-forward another two decades and the wheel choices are almost staggering.

Opposite: **Joker Machine's wheels can, by design, be mated to the company's brake rotors and drive pulleys with similar styling. This provides a unified appearance and an extra measure of "trick."**

There are cast aluminum, billet aluminum, hybrids, wheels made from sheet material, and, of course, the ever-durable spoke wheel.

Something similar has happened to Harley brakes through the marque's lifetime. Early bikes had their forerunner's bicycle-style, internal-expanding drum brakes, hardly enough to arrest the speed of a bicycle, to say nothing of bringing one of those newfangled powered cycles to a halt. In time, the drums grew, sprouting larger drums and shoes, and were fitted with ever more complex methods of articulation. And then, almost out of the blue, the 1970s brought the disk brake into nearly overnight orthodoxy. At first, single disks graced each wheel, and by the end of the decade, the sportier models were displaying dual disks up front.

You could say we've come a long way.

Above: **Harley's stock cast-disk wheel is standard on the Fat Boy but can be fitted to any of the Softails. Many riders opt for polishing or chroming the normally black- or silver-painted wheel.**

Left: **American Wire Wheel makes a wide variety of spoke wheels, offered with chrome or stainless spokes and on aluminum or steel rims. Steel is tougher but heavier, and the chrome is easier to care for. Sporting riders—and those wanting racebike authenticity—go for the aluminum hoops.**

Harley's stock rear brakes for almost the entire line use single-piston calipers mated to a massive floating carrier. The carrier slides into a boss on the swingarm. Keep the locating pins clean and well greased for optimum braking action.

Braking Essentials

Braking is all about dissipating energy. Modern disk brakes take the energy from the velocity of the motorcycle and turn it into heat by means of friction. As the composite-material brake pads squeeze a brake disk, tremendous heat is liberated. That's why braking components have to be of high quality to be durable.

Any brake's power is determined by several parameters. First is the coefficient of friction between the pads and the disk. Second is the leverage used to press those pads against the disk. Third is the swept area of the pads, or the slice of the brake rotor that the pads touch. Fourth is the leverage upon the wheel from this swept area, which is determined by the diameter of the disk.

Harley's Tech

In universal use in the Harley line, the company's Hayes-manufactured, single-piston, single-action caliper is rugged, simple, and relatively inexpensive to build. It's just not very powerful, particularly noticeable on the heavier bikes. In addition, Harley fits disks of moderate size—11.5 inches in diameter up front—considering the size of the bikes. And until 1996, the company's engineering philosophies of sizing the master cylinder to the caliper resulted in a hard brake lever that, particularly in the single-disk applications, almost couldn't lock the front wheel. Braking is like money: You almost can't have too much.

Harley, to be fair, says flatly that it receives little complaint from the field about the quality of its braking systems. "It's just not on the list of gripes," says one Harley engineer.

So to increase braking efficiency, you must increase one or all of those parameters—swept area, pad area, hydraulic leverage, and wheel leverage (through larger-diameter rotors). Most aftermarket brakes increase braking power by fitting calipers that use larger pads and more actuating pistons than the stock setup.

Pistons, Pistons Everywhere

Harley's stock brakes use single pistons on a sliding caliper; the piston pushes one pad directly against the disk. Once this disk makes contact, any further movement comes from the caliper moving sideways, bringing the inboard pad with it.

All the popular aftermarket brakes are what's called dual action. That is, they use a separate piston on each side of the caliper, individually pushing a pad against the disk. Because there's no delay getting the inboard pad onto the disk, this type of caliper generally offers better, more rapid activation. Also, it's more likely that the dual-action caliper will wear its pads evenly than is true of the single-action types. A dual-action caliper also gets the manufacturer around having to design a sliding mechanism. On the other side of that coin is the fact that a dual-action caliper must be properly shimmed so that its centerline is along the centerline of the disk. If either component is offset, the pads may drag or there may be contact between the caliper structure and the disk.

Left: Arlen Ness created this caliper's cosmetics and has Performance Machine build it. Four pistons act on rectangular pads. Here, the caliper is mated to a polished Harley Parts & Accessories floating disk.

Below: Employed for the past decade-plus, the single-action Kelsey-Hayes caliper uses semicircular pads of a fairly hard compound for long life. Softer, aftermarket pads represent a big improvement for the stock brakes, although for ultimate performance, aftermarket brake components are better.

1. Stock Harleys come with 16-, 19-, or 21-inch front wheels. Custom bikes like this Bartels' FXR may end up with 17-inch wheels and big brakes. While this setup looks great, it's unlikely that the bike will have the same docile handling qualities as a stocker. In general, wildly different wheel sizes and widths cause unusual handling qualities on stock-framed bikes. No doubt, with so much brake, this custom stops well.

2. Dressing up the stock components by chroming or polishing is common. Notice, though, the smear marks made by the pad during normal use. There's no way to keep a polished rotor pristine and still use it for braking.

Early dual-action calipers had just two pistons, one on each side of the disk. In time, the orthodoxy on racing bikes became the four-piston caliper. Essentially, the four-piston caliper allows the pad area to be concentrated near the outer radius of the disk while still maintaining sufficient total pad area for good durability; this concentration gives the pads greater leverage on the wheel and therefore better stopping ability. Taking this philosophy one step further is the six-piston caliper, now popular in racing circles and making good headway into the custom-Harley market.

3. A chromed caliper often makes a good contrast to a blacked-out fork assembly, as on this Springer. It's mated to Harley's floating disk with black center.

4. Polishing or chroming the caliper requires care because contaminants from the polishing process can harm the internal seals, so many riders elect to leave the caliper black and polish the disk only. Note the smearing of the polished disk surface; it's inevitable.

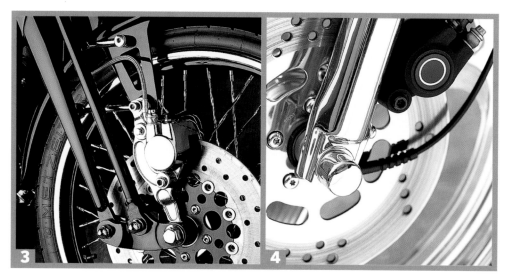

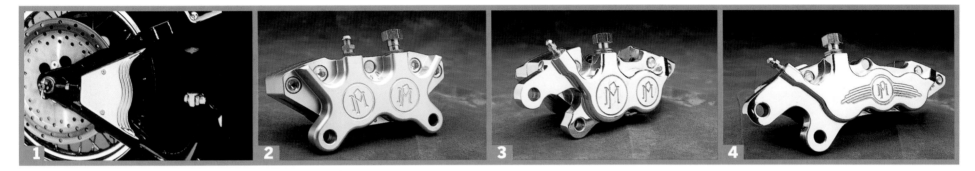

The Players

Performance Machine has established itself as a frontrunner among Harley brake makers. Its catalog lists a wide variety of two-, four-, and six-piston calipers, brake rotors, and mounting schemes.

Two things make PM's brakes stand out. First, they are all CNC-machined, which should give them an advantage over cast competitors because they are more rigid. (Admittedly, most current high-end calipers are also CNC'd these days.) PM also makes calipers in different sizes for dual- and single-disk applications, for compact arrangements that make room for spoke wheels, and with integral mounting tabs.

Simple bolt-on calipers are relatively new. For many years, Harley customizers had to fabricate their own brackets because the calipers in use weren't made for Harleys. Now PM, among several others, makes calipers with the mounting bosses as part of the structure. One big benefit is that there are fewer pieces, plus the installation is much cleaner this way. The only real downside is that you can't later upgrade to larger-diameter brake rotors without trading the calipers. (With the

caliper/bracket combos, all you need to do is change the bracket.)

Custom Chrome has its own line of four-piston calipers, too. Based on a quartet of 1.25-inch-diameter pistons, this basic caliper is offered with integral mounting ears for front-wheel use, or with brackets to work at the rear of the bike. The internals are the same. (Custom Chrome warns that these calipers are not compatible with Harley P&A's floating rotors.) Custom Chrome is also distributing a six-piston caliper from Harrison Engineering in England under the Billet-6 name; it requires that you make your own bracket.

Another player is GMA, out of Omaha, Nebraska. It offers three basic caliper families, in two- and four-piston configurations. Like the PM and Custom Chrome offerings, GMA has front calipers with integrated brackets.

Storz Performance is the sole distributor of the Grimeca line of brakes, made in Italy. Of note is the company's cast six-piston caliper. It's both fairly light and rigid, but also a surprisingly good deal at about half the cost of top-line calipers.

1. If you don't want to replace the brakes, try covering them up. Custom Chrome's Softail brake caliper cover fits between the swingarm tubes to conceal the stock caliper.

2. PM's longest-lived, most popular caliper is the 125X4, with twin pistons on each side of the caliper gripping one-piece pads. (Some of the six-piston brakes use individual pads for each puck.)

3. Performance Machine's four-piston differential-bore caliper. By placing the smaller-bore piston on the leading edge of the caliper, the pressure across the pad is equalized, resulting in better pad life and more uniform braking.

4. Taking the pistons to the next increment is the PM differential-bore six-piston caliper. Each of the three pistons on each side of the caliper is a different diameter.

1. **GMA's billet front caliper uses four equal-size pistons acting on one-piece pads. This bike uses the older 10.75-inch rotors. This model employs an aluminum bracket to mate the caliper to the fork leg. GMA also makes a version of this caliper whose mounting lugs match those of the stock Harley fork.**

2. **GMA's two-piston rear caliper grips an 11.5-inch ductile iron rotor. It's not necessary to have huge, quad-piston calipers at the rear of the bike because the foot pedal gives sufficient leverage to make just about any caliper work adequately. Some radical customs have six-piston calipers on the rear wheel, which is a fair bit of overkill.**

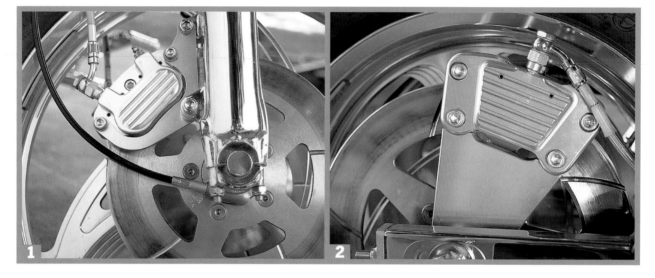

It requires a separate mounting bracket, but Storz will sell you one.

It's difficult to judge from the catalogs and specifications which aftermarket caliper is the best deal for you, but here are a few guidelines:

• Try to buy the lightest caliper in your price range. Divining between heavy enough to be stiff—a major consideration for a caliper— and needlessly overbuilt is difficult.

• An exception to the above for touring riders: You need a rugged brake system that can absorb some real heat. An extra pound or two on the wheel is a small price to pay for more durability.

• Look for calipers that can be easily rebuilt. Every caliper uses a seal between the hydraulic cavity and the exposed portion of the piston.

Be sure you can get the rebuilt kits easily, because sooner or later you'll need them.

• Buy what you need. Let's face it. A pair of six-piston calipers on 13-inch disks make for great stoppers. But if you're running a 21-inch front wheel, there will not be enough contact patch with that 2.15-inch-wide tire to use all that stopping power. A single four-piston caliper is an improvement over stock without going way beyond what the front tire can handle.

Thinking in hydraulics

When you retrofit brakes, bear a few things in mind. How a brake feels at the lever or foot pedal has a great deal to do with hydraulic leverage. The master cylinder uses a small-diameter piston to move a small amount of fluid at great pressure.

At the caliper, this pressure is turned back into displacement of the pistons and brake pads.

A very large master cylinder piston and a very small caliper piston will result in a very stiff lever that is capable of moving a lot of fluid but at a relatively low pressure. It would take herculean strength to lock the front tire of a bike so set up.

Conversely, a very small master cylinder piston and a large caliper piston will net a brake that is very powerful with the slightest pull at the lever; but to activate the brakes fully, you might use all the available lever travel. Moreover, this brake will feel mushy.

Such are the compromises. Remember that the stock caliper, even with a single large piston, has relatively little piston area. Substitute a four-piston caliper, and the braking force will increase and the lever effort will go down. Use the same master cyl-

inder and add a second four-piston caliper, and the result will be an unacceptably mushy lever, although the brakes are likely to be quite powerful.

It pays, then, to listen to the manufacturer's recommendations regarding master-cylinder size. Generally speaking, you can substitute a single four-piston caliper (or one of PM's smaller six-piston calipers) for the stock single caliper without changing master cylinders. But if you have dual

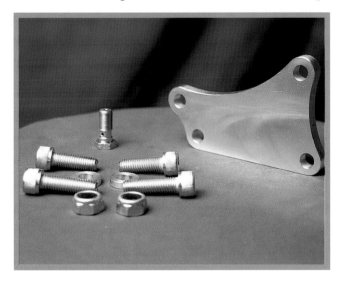

Above: Harley's late-model master cylinders come in two basic bore sizes depending on whether the bike originally had single or dual front brakes. Pre-1996 bikes had overall larger bore sizes, which result in a slightly wooden brake feel. A move to additional brake calipers will reduce lever pressure but may result in a spongy lever feel.

Left: Many of the aftermarket calipers—particularly those designed for other types of bikes—require adapting hardware, like this solid aluminum plate for the Grimeca caliper. Be sure to use good-quality hardware and to apply a thread locker.

Inside Performance Machine

Performance Machine is arguably an overdog in the world of Harley wheels and brakes. It was founded in 1970 as a one-person operation by Perry Sands. Sands, then a professional machinist, says that founding the company came from necessity. "I had a need for good machined parts because I was building bikes," Sands says. "My first custom was an Indian, and then I built a lot of customer bikes. One of my specializations was to build Springer front ends from scratch." At the time, Sands was working in someone else's shop and using the equipment after hours. Eventually, he sold a number of personal items, including his truck, to finance a "lathe, welder, drill press, and a few other odds and ends," says Sands.

From a start in his own garage, Sands moved into an old dairy building in 1972; he hired a part-time employee then. Along with the bike work, Sands was doing the usual shop work. In the years to come, Sands helped build a number of customs and then, he says, brakes got to be an issue. There were no other serious options for aftermarket brakes, so Sands began casting a rear master cylinder and, later, a caliper of his own design. He claims to have built the first for-motorcycle-use two-piston caliper.

In 1980, Sands bought an early CNC lathe and a few months later bought a CNC mill. (Remember, this was before cheap, powerful computers.) "We used the CNC machinery expressly for building motorcycle components," Sands says. "We built wire-wheel hubs with that equipment, and looked at the parts we were casting and said, 'Wait a minute—we can build this stuff on CNC.' So we did. We were the first in the motorcycle industry to use this equipment." Sands reckons his company was about five years ahead of the other aftermarketers in using CNC equipment.

From the few initial products, the Performance Machine line grew. Two-piston calipers started the line, but

four-piston jobs soon came along and later the current top-line six-piston calipers. Today, PM has a large variety of calipers in these configurations. Some of the calipers are designed to bolt right onto the stock Harley fork leg, while others, for example, require an adapter bracket. (One advantage of the bracket method is that if you want to go to a larger brake rotor, you don't

1. Performance Machine calipers begin life as solid chunks of aluminum. First, the profile is cut from stock, then subsequent machining processes begin to define the shape. PM installs these blanks in racks so the CNC machine can work on several sets at a time.

2. Calipers that have been through all the machining processes are inspected and then fitted with pistons and seals. All are leak-checked before they are packaged for shipment.

have to toss the caliper itself; just make a new bracket.)

On the current rage of everything-from-billet accessory builders, Sands comments, "There are really two ways you can use CNC machinery to make billet components. You can do it quick and dirty. Or you can use some 'nice moves' to generate smooth radiuses and curves and three-axis contours. Which takes more time, but you end up with a much nicer part."

Sands says, "A big issue when you're dealing with hydraulics is quality control. A lot of other brake makers are farming the pieces out to machine shops, and that makes it hard to keep a firm grip on the quality."

At the beginning of 1998, Sands and company—populated by several family members, incidentally—picked up stakes from its Paramount, California, location and moved to bigger digs in La Palma, California. The

company's twenty CNC machines and 110 employees all made the move without incident. Sands hopes the larger facility will enable the company to tackle the one thing that most dogs it—the inability to fulfill all orders as quickly as Sands would like. "We were, in some ways, a victim of our own success," he says.

An interesting side note to the Performance Machine story is that its Image line of calipers—a largely fashion-driven design—has been unceremoniously dropped after just a year. "We found that it didn't sell well, and we felt that it was too much of a compromise—too heavy and expensive for the performance increase." It's a telling assessment, one that most manufacturers in the Harley aftermarket would be reluctant to disclose. But it hints at the core of PM's enduring success—make the product work right, keep the quality up, and the rest will take care of itself.

3. Computer machining is used for many steps in the production of PM's billet wheels. In some cases, the entire wheel is cut from billet by the machines, while other models use the CNC mills to set the critical clearances between the hub and bearings.

4. A completed wheel center emerges from the CNC machine, ready to be mated with an extruded rim and then sent to the polishing shop.

5. Perry Sands started Performance Machine from humble origins and has, with the help of several family members, turned the company into a major force in the Harley aftermarket.

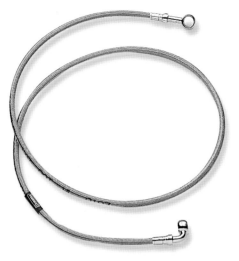

Left: Harley's **P&A** department sells a set of braided-steel lines for most models; they are direct bolt-on replacements for the stock rigid-and-rubber lines.

Below: Harley will also sell you the same spoke wheels that are about a $300 option popular on current models. They use steel rims and zinc-plated spokes. Be sure you buy the proper front wheel; some of the hubs have provisions for just one brake, while another part number may accommodate dual disks.

1. Along with a polished rotor, you can polish or chrome the caliper for a fully bright wheel assembly. Springer front ends are normally shod with just one caliper and disk. It takes a custom-made caliper carrier and front wheel to convert a Springer to dual disks.

2. Polished disks look great when new but will eventually smear under normal usage.

3. PM's fixed, or one-piece, rotors are available in stock 11.5-inch diameters as well as the 13-inch size. They are less complicated than the floating rotors but cannot handle the same heat load before warping. Fortunately, the braking demands of most customs are well below this threshold.

Harley calipers, you'll need to go to a larger-diameter master cylinder. (If the aftermarket caliper has twice the piston area as the stocker, you're only doubling the leverage ratio with the single-caliper swap, but you're quadrupling it with the dual-caliper exchange.)

Disk Options

If you believe the customizers, Harley's stamped stainless rotors aren't much to look at. That's probably why you see so many brake disks exchanged or modified for appearance' sake.

Until recently, there were not many aftermarket Harley disks, so most customizers resorted to polishing or chroming the stock items. Doing so ignores the tenet of good braking: Friction equals power. By polishing the surface of the disk, its coefficient of friction is reduced considerably. Moreover, byproducts of the polishing process are often left behind in the surface of the rotor, only to contaminate the pads. Worse yet is chroming. The surface finish of chrome is very slick, and many riders discover to their dismay that a chrome disk leaves precious little braking power.

It seems that many riders have not only discovered this quirk but have learned from it, because the trend now is toward traditional stainless rotors with shiny center sections, or carriers. It's possible with two-piece or floating rotors to have a trick design on the carrier that will not impair the function of the rotor itself.

Rotors come in fixed or floating configurations. Harley uses a fixed system stock, and there are plenty of aftermarket fixed rotors to choose from. There's basically nothing wrong with a fixed disk for modest braking needs, and the payback comes in simplicity and economy.

But floating disks are the hot item today, a trickle-down from the racing ranks. Because the brake rotor has to dissipate a great amount of heat, it expands significantly. Unfortunately, not all of the disk has to dissipate the same amount of heat; the center section, away from the fiery pads, has relatively little to contend with. So, as will any metal heated unevenly, a fixed disk warps under hard use.

Floating rotors join a center carrier and the rotor proper with rivets. This scheme allow for some expansion without warping, and even allows some flexibility in the axial alignment of the disk and caliper.

Just as surface finish influences the coefficient of friction of the rotor, so too does its basic composition. Most popular of the materials is stainless steel, mainly because it's easy to work with and does not discolor with use and exposure to the elements. But it does not have the highest coefficient of friction. That's the cast-iron rotor. Performance Machine and GMA both make iron-rotor brakes that are better performers than stainless

1. Harley makes a floater version of its **OEM** disks, with either black or chromed centers. They are relatively inexpensive.

2. Floating disks rely on these steel buttons to carry the shearing forces. If your floater has too much side play, road vibration and normal braking will accelerate the wear on the buttons. Inspect the disks at every major service interval.

items. But you have to live with the rusting that's so common with iron rotors; this is not a performance problem, just an eyesore.

Not all floating disks are compatible with the standard Harley caliper, and some aftermarket calipers cannot be used with Harley's P&A floater.

Size Matters

Recent Harleys come stock with 11.5-inch rotors front and rear. Most of the aftermarket disks can be ordered in this diameter, but several also come in 10-inch or 13-inch sizes. The 10-inch rotors are great for retrofitting earlier bikes whose forks do not allow the now-standard 11.5-inch disk. While upping to the 13-inch size doesn't seem like much, the effect on braking is dramatic. You must ascertain that your aftermarket caliper will work with the larger disk—remember the outer radius will be different.

Pad Dynamics

If your head spins looking at all the brake components in the catalogs, wait until you see all the brake-pad possibilities. Even if you're intent on keeping the stock Harley system on your bike, you can improve the stopping power noticeably with aftermarket pads. Dunlopad, Ferodo, Galfer, and SBS all make high-end pads that provide greater friction for better stops, albeit at the expense of pad life. (Stock Harley pads are quite hard and seem to last forever.)

Just be sure to match the pad type to the disk material. Polished or chromed disks should use only organic pads, never metallic or semimetallic. (These coarser pads will chew up the finish in short order.) If you still have the stock stainless disks, you can choose from any number of semimetallic, Kevlar, ceramic, or carbon-fiber composites.

Finally, always pay attention to the break-in procedures specified by the pad maker. Some pads

like a hard, fast break-in, while others will be damaged unless the first few stops are gentle.

Each pad manufacturer makes compounds that range from very soft to quite hard. The main difference here is the tradeoff between long life and the pad's coefficient of friction. The softer pad will provide more aggressive braking but at the expense of longevity. As a rule, you should opt for the softer pad compounds for lightweight bikes and the midrange compounds for the baggers. Also, buy softer pads for the front than for the rear. Harley's rear brakes have plenty of leverage and power, so you don't gain much by going to a softer (greater gripping) pad. Make it a point to inspect

the pads every oil change to avoid nasty noises—the grinding of a pad backing plate into the disk sounds a lot like the *ka-ching* of a cash register, doesn't it?

The Wheel Thing

Today, there are more options to changing the look of your wheels than simply modifying the ones you have. (Even so, chroming, painting, or highlighting the stock wheels remains very popular.) Replacement wheels come in a wide variety of shapes, construction methods, and sizes. Let's look at the basics.

High-Wire Act

Historically significant and widely loved by Harley-philes around the world, the workhorse wire wheel is still a strong seller. Harley now offers wire wheels as an option on every bike it sells, and a good many buyers check that box on the sales sheet.

Above: Larger rotors, like this 13-inch Image from PM, offer better braking and may be used in a single- or dual-disk installation. Small buttons between the center carrier and disk allow for expansion and help prevent warping.

Left: Performance Machine builds a line of wheels in both billet and cast, using in many cases the same designs. Cast wheels are generally less expensive but can be heavier.

"A radial-spoke wheel can be damaged by hard acceleration or very hard braking. This is a clear case of style taking precedence over function."

Spoke wheels are tremendously strong for their weight, offering by far the best strength-to-weight ratio of any motorcycle wheel around. Traditional wheels have forty spokes laced in tension; that is, the spokes distribute the wheel loads along the length of the spokes. Ideally, there's no twisting or shearing force applied to the spokes. Radial-spoke wheels, where the spokes are mounted in bending, have been but a blip on the Harley radar screen—for good reason. Because the radial-spoke wheel can't absorb the load in the same plane as where the spoke is most strong, every part of the wheel must be stronger and therefore heavier to resist the shear forces imposed on the spokes. Moreover, even when radically overbuilt, a radial-spoke wheel can be damaged by the excessive twisting forces imparted by hard acceleration or very hard braking. This is a clear case of style taking precedence over function.

Various materials are used in spoke wheels. Harley currently uses steel rims with chromed aluminum hubs and zinc-plated spokes. The steel rims are the strongest option for spoke wheels; they endure minor road encounters with less chance of bending or denting than aluminum-rim wheels. On the other hand, aluminum rims are about one-third lighter. (More on the weight-versus-strength compromise later.) A good, steel-rim laced wheel for a Harley weighs between 12 and 17 pounds.

Aftermarket wheels may use any number of materials in combination. Most wheel makers sell steel rims to the Harley market because the riders have voted in that direction. Several manufacturers have begun making the hubs out of billet aluminum. Harley uses a casting, as do several other wheel manufacturers. In theory, the billet piece would be stronger and more durable, but the hub usually isn't the wheel's weak link. Buy billet because it makes you feel better, rather than to expect longer wheel life.

Both alloy and steel rims are made from extrusions cut and bent into a circle. There's a small weld where the extruded rim section meets itself to complete the circle.

How Many Spokes You Want?

A recent trend has been toward more and more spokes. Eighty, 120, even 160 spokes on a wheel are not uncommon. Doubling or tripling the number of spokes helps distribute the load of acceleration into smaller and smaller bits, making life easier on the spokes. And while these wheels undoubtedly look better, the mechanical advantages are somewhat specious. Only for the most breathed-on monster bike is the standard 40-spoke rear wheel a marginal item.

Naturally, more spokes, more weight. Moreover, these spoke-sprouting wheels will be more difficult to maintain and clean than a traditional 40-spoke model. Keep these considerations in mind.

There are usually several choices in spoke material—zinc-plated steel, chromed steel, and stainless steel. Here's a simple answer: Always go stainless. Chrome is slightly easier to wash and keep shiny, but inevitably water will get under the chrome around the nipple head and begin to corrode its surface. Next thing, you have flaking

Left: A once-popular trend was toward radial-spoke wheels. Today, the radial-spoke wheel is still popular for front fitments, but because it has a difficult time transmitting the torque of the engine to the ground, few rear-wheel applications are offered.

Below: Large front wheels practically cry out for more spokes. This Arlen Ness 21-inch front wheel's 80 spokes are an exercise in high style, but plan to spend the better part of an hour truing and maintaining a megaspoke wheel.

Wheel truing is not a lost art, but the professionals, like those at Buchanan's, take advantage of purpose-built truing stands. You can get most of the benefits right in your own garage using a motorcycle lift and some patience.

chrome everywhere. Harley's stock wheels use the zinc plating, and they look fine for the first couple of years. But they will eventually discolor, and there's nothing you can do to repair the finish that doesn't require either a lot of handiwork or disassembly of the rim.

Here it is again: Save yourself the headaches and go stainless.

So laced wheels are great—they look the way motorcycle wheels should, they're light and strong, and they're relatively inexpensive. (Harley's own aftermarket spoke wheels are some 30 percent cheaper than similar-size cast wheels, for example.) But there are some downsides.

Maintenance. Yep, you have to do some. Buchanan's Wheel Works, a premier wire-wheel manufacturer, recommends an initial tightening between 500 and 1000 miles after a spoke wheel is built—the company says to just give each nipple a quarter turn. It also suggests an examination every year for missing or loose spokes, cracks in the hub and wheel, and to determine if the inner tube and stem are seated properly. Properly measuring wheel true and maintaining the spokes requires you to either jack up the bike or remove the wheels and place them in a stand. You can perform basic spoke maintenance with the wheels on the bike, and the bike on the sidestand, but it's much more work and chances are you won't do a good a job.

Cleaning. Another serious downside. Nobody enjoys an afternoon of wire-wheel cleansing. It's a bear to get every spoke, every flat of the rim and hub, and every nipple clean and shiny. No doubt—you will pay at every washing for the classic looks and light weight of a laced wheel.

Inner tubes. From a performance standpoint, the need for an inner tube is probably the biggest shortcoming of the wire wheel. Automobiles and aircraft early on got away from laced wheels and inner tubes because the tube creates additional heat in high-speed and high-load applications. Moreover, a tube-type tire is more likely to have a sudden loss of pressure than a tubeless tire; again, an important item for cars and airplanes. Motorcycles, too, for that matter.

Cast Wheels Bow

Other forms of transportation embraced the tubeless tire thanks to solid steel wheels. For motorcycles, the turning point came in the late 1970s with the introduction of the cast "mag" wheel. Early versions for racing were indeed magnesium, in part for its very light weight. But magnesium is a difficult material to work with, prone to unseen corrosion that can radically impair the strength of the part. So as a solution, wheel makers began to use cast aluminum as the hub and spokes of this new kind of wheel.

There are several ways to cast a wheel. Typically, a permanent mold is used for the center section, into which molten aluminum is poured. A good mold will allow controlled cooling rates as this aluminum sets, which helps keep porosity and density within desired limits. Another way to cast the wheel is to inject the liquid aluminum into a mold that has a vacuum; this suction helps move the aluminum and draw away the gases during the set cycle. Finally, there's die casting, in which sheets of aluminum are pressed in precision dies to achieve the desired form.

Usually, a central aluminum casting mates to an extruded or spun rim that can be welded or bolted together. Castings have come a long way since the early efforts, which were porous almost to the point of distraction and quite heavy. Now with die casting, investment casting, and computer-controlled machining processes, the cast wheel can come close to the overall weight of a laced wheel. (Close, but still no match.)

Of prime importance to users of the cast wheel is the ability to run tubeless tires. (Some wire wheels are designed to go tubeless, but few of those—notably the designs in which the spoke nipple doesn't penetrate the rim extrusion—have been successful.) Now, with less heat to dissipate, the tire could be lighter and more flexible without losing strength.

1. Twisted spokes add a bit of spice to otherwise ordinary spoke wheels, but they have the tendency to "unwind" themselves under hard use. Just make sure to check the tightness of the spokes after the initial 500 or 1000 miles and at every oil change thereafter.

2. Another slant on the spoke theme is the diamond-shape or "waisted" spoke. They look great but require additional material to make the shapes possible, which adds slightly to the weight of the wheel.

3. Chroming of standard Harley wheels is quite common and an inexpensive way to dress up the bike; here is the standard Fat Boy front disk wheel in chrome.

Joker Machine's billet wheels are intentionally made heavy and strong because, as the company says, "That's what Harley riders want."

Cast wheels have some other advantages:

Maintenance. None to speak of, save for the occasional inspection for cracks and other normal wheel maladies.

Cleaning. Piece of cake. Hose them off and you're done.

Easy customizing. Although it's certainly possible to customize laced wheels with anodized rims and hubs, thanks to the reduced parts count, it's far easier to paint, polish, or chrome cast wheels. One important warning applies: Cast wheels even today are porous. It takes a truly good chrome shop to get the plating to stick to some cast wheels, particularly the stock Harley items, which are fairly porous by industry standards. There may be substantial additional work required to chrome these wheels properly.

Billet Wheels

A newcomer on the frontier is the billet wheel, which, as the name implies, is cut from a solid block of aluminum. Billet is popular for manufacturing for a couple of reasons. First, it's extremely strong, coming as it does from a chunk of extruded aluminum, whose density and porosity are easily known and wonderfully consistent. Second, producing from billet means that a change of design requires only the reprogramming of the CNC machine, not a new mold. It's for this reason that Harley has kept the same wheel families in production for so long; to change the mold or die is expensive. Billet is expensive because you leave more raw aluminum on the floor next to the machine than can be found on the finished part.

Some aftermarket billet wheels are in fact hybrids. One manufacturer might use extruded and bent rims welded or bolted to a machined-from-

1. Another of Performance Machine's designs uses the precision of CNC machining to make tight, short-radius designs possible on the face of the spokes. This wheel style, like many of PM's, is available for both front and rear applications in stock and larger-than-standard widths.

2. Pencil spokes are a classic chopper style.

3. Radical designs, like this PM "flamed" style wheel, are eye-catching, but you must understand that any metal on the wheel that doesn't strictly hold it together is just adding weight.

4. PM's eagle wheel is entirely CNC machined, with 14,000 individual tool passes. This photo shows the wheel in the as-machined state prior to polishing.

block center section. Another manufacturer might build the rim from a solid circle of material that has been "spun" on CNC machinery. Other solid wheels might have sheet aluminum cut to size on computer equipment and then welded or bolted to the rim.

Finally, in the wake of the staggering popularity of solid billet wheels (discussed next), many aftermarket companies have begun producing cast wheels that have the look and feel of billet. Because most of these are polished or chromed, they have many of the advantages of billet wheels in terms of surface finish, while not being quite as expensive.

Weight versus Performance

CNC-machined billet wheels and high-tech cast wheels have the appearance riders want—that's not in question—but many manufacturers let the weight of these pieces get out of hand. Particularly in the case of cast wheels designed to look like CNC'd parts, the wheel can get quite heavy indeed. (It's not uncommon to find 20- to 25-pound wheels in the aftermarket.) This is because the casting does not have the strength of the billet piece, even after heat treating, so the wheel elements must be heavier and thicker to maintain strength.

Truth is, the vast majority of aftermarket Harley wheels are dramatically overbuilt.

Why would this ever be a problem?

Heavy wheels impose several performance limitations because they increase the total weight of the bike as well as, perhaps more importantly, the unsprung weight of each wheel. (Unsprung weight is the weight of the wheel, tire, brake, and suspension components on the axle side of the suspension. Half the suspension pieces like springs, dampers, and swingarm are considered unsprung weight. All other weight is considered sprung.)

Here's why unsprung weight is an important consideration.

Suspension compliance. Increasing unsprung weight makes it more difficult for the wheel to follow the road and in turn makes the suspension system work much harder. Ride quality suffers, particularly over small pavement imperfections, with heavy wheels.

Acceleration. A heavy wheel resists changes in speed more than a lighter one, so your bike will not brake or accelerate as well with heavy wheels. Heavy wheels act like huge flywheels, storing energy that becomes difficult to dissipate through braking.

Handling. Heavy wheels also create a stronger gyroscopic effect, the very thing that keeps a bike from falling over at speed. With more gyro effect, a bike will be less willing to lean over for cornering, although it will feel more stable in a straight line. Unfortunately, a bike with lots of gyroscopic influence will, once deflected from the desired course, want to continue in that direction.

Component stress. Wheels that are excessively heavy will also create greater loads on bearings and bushings, the steering head, and the

1. **CNC machining makes all sorts of shapes possible, but a well-designed wheel will have just enough material to be strong but not so much that it becomes excessively heavy. Portly wheels harm ride quality.**

2. **Aftermarket wheels are normally set up like the stock hub, for belt drive and Harley-compatible brake components.**

swingarm pivot. Not only that, but you'll be using your brakes harder to make the same kinds of stops as before the wheel swap.

So the reasons are compelling to shoot for the lightest wheels you can find of a given design and style. Unfortunately, most wheel manufacturers fail to make weight information easily available. Your best bet is to go to your local speed shop and heft one in person.

Buying Tips

Before you plunk down for a sweet-looking set of wheels, be sure you check candidate wheels for the following characteristics:

Established brands. Watch the magazine ads and you'll see a new wheel company arrive one month and be gone a year later. Because wheels are popular, high-markup items, they attract many new players every year. But to protect your investment, longtime customizers recommend only buying from established brands, such as Akront, American Wire Wheel, Excel, Hallcraft's, Performance Machine, RC Components, and the

like. Moreover, many of the big distributors like Custom Chrome, Drag Specialties, and Nempco each have house brands; because the distributor will probably be around even if the subcontractor building the wheels has gone under, you're protected.

Does that mean shy away from anyone but the established makers? Not necessarily; just understand that you're walking out on a thinner limb.

Finish. Particularly for chromed cast wheels, make sure the plating is smooth and without bubbles, cracks, or nicks. The rejection rate is quite high on chromed cast parts, so don't be surprised to see a few sets of imperfect wheels at your local Harley haven. Reject any imperfectly finished wheel unless you can get a sizable discount.

Axial run-out. This term simply describes how true the wheel is from side to side. Place the wheel on a plate-glass counter and you'll be able to get a fair idea of whether the wheel tracks well. Wheel with excessive axial run-out will wobble at speed and may even make contact with parts of the motorcycle.

Above: **Rowe's truing stand is a useful workshop tool if your bike has laced wheels. The bench-top stand makes truing and balancing far easier than on the bike.**

Opposite: **This wild custom wears a complete billet ensemble, including Performance Machine billet, bolt-together wheels and matching pulley, an Arlen Ness belt guard and FXR-style fender rail with integral marker lights, and Delta Fournales shocks.**

Radial run-out. The same idea, only applied to how well the rim traces a constant radius around the axle. This is a harder measurement to make unless you can get the wheel put on a balancing stand. Accept between .005 inch and .010 inch of axial or radial run-out. Remember, too, that for spoke wheels, any side-to-side variation or out-of-roundness can be easily remedied.

Bearings. Most wheels on the shelves today come with high-quality Timken bearings. Be wary of imported counterparts; time has shown them to be inferior to the American-made part.

Mounting and balancing of tires. Inevitably, you'll have to put some tires on those shiny new wheels. Make certain that the tire is mounted properly. Many premium tires are directional, so look for the direction arrow molded into the sidewall. Don't accept a salesman's word that the direction doesn't matter—it does. Also, be looking to see that the tire changer puts the tire in place with the painted dot positioned at the valve stem. This dot is the lightest part of the tire and needs to be aligned with the heaviest part of the rim. Doing so will help reduce the amount of balancing weight needed. Be sure to have the tire and wheel dynamically spin balanced. You can get close with static bench balancing, but if you have it available, go dynamic. Finally, double-check for proper inflation pressures. Many tire changers use some 60 PSI to seat the bead and forget to drop the pressure afterward; your bike will ride like Barney Rubble's wagon if you forget, too.

Sizes. Aftermarket wheels are available in several sizes. Stock Harleys use a combination of these rim sizes: 2.15x21, 2.15x9, and 3.00x16. You can generally increase rim width by $1/2$ inch without worrying about running shy of clearances. Unfortunately, beyond that rule of thumb, there are few absolutes. Especially if you have lowered the bike and also changed fenders, there's no guarantee that any tire and wheel combo will fit. Many customizers swap the chunky 16-inch rear tire present on all Harleys with lower-profile 17- or 18-inch models. Do this only if you can see and touch another bike that has successfully made the switch; again, there are too many variables to say here whether any given wheel and tire combo will fit into a stock-framed bike.

Part of a switch to a larger-diameter rear tire is often a move to a radial tire. Harley doesn't recommend this change, with good reason. The Harley chassis are not designed and tested with radials, so handling qualities may deteriorate with them in place. A radial tire is constructed so differently from a bias-ply tire (which all Harleys carry from the factory) that there's no assurance it won't turn your bike into an ill-handling beast.

Epilogue

Accessorizing your Harley will give you not just a distinctive motorcycle but also a tremendous sense of pride and personal accomplishment. Once you've made your changes, you'll sneak a look back at your bike every time you walk away from it. It's the kind of satisfaction you just don't get from other hobbies, in part because your results are almost instantaneous. Bolt on a part, change the exhaust system, relocate your turn signals—and the results are there to see, feel, and enjoy.

Throughout your journey of customizing, keep a few basic thoughts in mind. Remember that this is *your* motorcycle. Don't let the tastes of the parts guy at the dealership or trends set in motion by famous customizers alter your vision of what your motorcycle should be. Modify intelligently. That means if you are perfectly happy with the performance of your Big Twin with a carb kit and a set of slip-ons, don't let the guy down the block with the 120-inch engine convince you otherwise.

Finally, some buying tips. Know the suggested retail prices of the items you intend to purchase. Though it's not so prevalent now, during the big boom of the early 1990s, it was common for shops to mark up prices beyond retail and knock them back down a smidgen to look like they were offering discounts. You should be able to find most items for suggested retail price, and in the case of closeouts, significantly less. Don't, however, expect deep discounts across the board—we're not talking about VCRs here.

Use your credit card. Most banking institutions provide a layer of consumer protection when you use a credit card that may come in handy if you get a defective part from a shop that's unwilling or unable to fix the problem to your satisfaction.

Custom work can be another matter. Most painters, for example, want cash on the barrel head when the project is complete. Any remedies after you take the part home may have to be agreed on by both of you.

Buy from established companies. It's true that there's a lot of wonderful work being done by small shops, firms with only a single product in their catalog, and offshoot companies that had previously been subcontractors for a larger company. But because there's so much variation in quality of materials and consistency of fit, you really need to know what you're getting. Until you can tell by touch and sight the quality of any given part, it's better to stay with the stable, well-known manufacturers and distributors.

Most of all, enjoy personalizing your motorcycle and making your Harley *yours*. Accessorizing is fun, slightly addictive, and certainly an endeavor you'll wish you'd started sooner.